Other Books and Series I

*1901-1907 Native American Census Seneca, Eas
Ottawa, Peoria, Quapaw, and Wyandotte Indians
Territory)*

*1932 Census of The Standing Rock Sioux Reserv.
1924-1932*

Census of The Blackfeet, Montana, 1897- 1901 Expanded Edition

Eastern Cherokee by Blood, 1906-1910, Volumes I thru XIII

*Choctaw of Mississippi Indian Census 1929-1932 with Births and Deaths 1924-
1931   Volume I*

*Choctaw of Mississippi Indian Census 1933, 1934 & 1937, Supplemental Rolls to
1934 & 1935 with Births and Deaths 1932-1938, and Marriages 1936-1938
Volume II*

*Eastern Cherokee Census Cherokee, North Carolina 1930-1939
Census 1930-1931 with Births And Deaths 1924-1931 Taken By Agent L. W. Page
Volume I*

*Eastern Cherokee Census Cherokee, North Carolina 1930-1939
Census 1932-1933 with Births And Deaths 1930-1932 Taken By Agent R. L.
Spalsbury   Volume II*

*Eastern Cherokee Census Cherokee, North Carolina 1930-1939
Census 1934-1937 with Births and Deaths 1925-1938 and Marriages 1936 & 1938
Taken by Agents R. L. Spalsbury And Harold W. Foght Volume III*

*Seminole of Florida Indian Census, 1930-1940 with Birth and Death
Records, 1930-1938*

Texas Cherokees 1820-1839 A Document For Litigation 1921

Choctaw By Blood Enrollment Cards 1898-1914 Volumes I thru XVII

*Starr Roll 1894 (Cherokee Payment Rolls) Districts: Canadian, Cooweescoowee,
and Delaware Volume One*

*Starr Roll 1894 (Cherokee Payment Rolls) Districts: Flint, Going Snake, and
Illinois   Volume Two*

*Starr Roll 1894 (Cherokee Payment Rolls) Districts: Saline, Sequoyah, and
Tahlequah; Including Orphan Roll Volume Three*

Other Books and Series by Jeff Bowen

Cherokee Intruder Cases Dockets of Hearings 1901-1909 Volumes I & II

Indian Wills, 1911-1921 Records of the Bureau of Indian Affairs
Books One thru Five

Visit our website at **www.nativestudy.com** to learn more about these
and other books and series by Jeff Bowen

INDIAN WILLS

RECORDS OF THE BUREAU OF INDIAN AFFAIRS

1911 - 1921

BOOK SIX

TRANSCRIBED BY

JEFF BOWEN

NATIVE STUDY
Gallipolis, Ohio
USA

Originally published:
Baltimore, Maryland
2007

Reprinted by:

Native Study LLC
Gallipolis, OH
www.nativestudy.com

Library of Congress Control Number: 2020915163

ISBN: 978-1-64968-031-0

Book cover photograph taken by Jeff Bowen, October, 1998, titled *Early Morning at Fort Toulouse*, where the Coosa and Tallapoosa Rivers meet, Wetumpka, Alabama.

Made in the United States of America.

INTRODUCTION

These documents were found in the *Guide to Records in the National Archives of the United States Relating to AMERICAN INDIANS* on page 98, "eight volumes of copies of Indian wills, 1911-21, that, pursuant to the act of 1910 and an act of February 13, 1913 (37 Stat. 678), were referred to the Bureau and the Office of the Secretary of the Interior for Approval."

The Native American wills and probate records were listed under, "RECORDS OF THE LAW AND PROBATE DIVISIONS." The Law and Probate Divisions evolved from the Land Division that handled legal matters until a separate law office was established in 1907. By 1911, this office was mostly called the Law Division. An act of June 25, 1910 (36 Stat. 855), authorized by the Secretary of the Interior, was to determine the heirs of deceased Indian trust allottees; both the Land Division and the Law Division handled work resulting from this legislation. In 1913, an Heirship Section was established in the land Division that later was mostly concerned with probate work. By 1917, the Division was usually called the Probate Division.

The wills themselves were never filmed until they were discovered by the author and filmed in 1996. The wills and probate records consisted of 2568 pages.

The wills are not numbered in any certain order; there are 181 pages of wills without index in this volume, consisting of approximately 101 different wills. The majority of the wills are of western origin and a few eastern ones that will be reproduced as more volumes are completed.

In *Book Two* there is one will that was actually taken to the highest office in the land, the President of the United States. Also one woman bequeathed to her husband her fishing location and two canoes.

Some of the tribes included among the wills are Sioux, Arickara, Apache, Comanche, Chippewa, Ukie and Wylackie, Omaha, Blackfoot, Squaxin band, Yuma, Cheyenne-Arapahoe, Siletz, Sac and Fox, Quinaielt, Crow, Iowa, Otoe and Missouria, Umatilla, Piegan, Klamath, and many more.

Jeff Bowen
Gallipolis, Ohio
NativeStudy.com

EDWIN GREEN

W I L L.

I, Edwin Green, of the Village of Odanah, in the County of Ashland, and State of Wisconsin, of the age of sixty-one (61) years, and being of sound and disposing mind and memory, do make, publish and declare, this my last will and Testament in manner following, that is to say:- To my grand-children, that they may share and share alike.

I give devise and bequeath, unto my grand-son Joseph E. Green, and unto my grand-daughter Agnes E. Green, each an undivided one-half of that certain piece or parcel of land, situated in the La Pointe Reservation, and described as the North-half of the North-west quarter of section twenty-five in Township forty-seven North of Range two west of the fourth Principal Meridian in Wisconsin; to have and to hold, to them, their heirs and assigns forever.

In witness whereof, I have hereunto set my hand and seal this second day of June, A.D. 1906.

Edwin Green (L.S.)

The foregoing instrument was at the date thereof signed, sealed, published and declared by the said testator, Edwin Green, as and for his last Will and Testament, in the presence of us, who at his request, in his presence and in the presence of each other have subscribed our names as witnesses thereto.

Kate Paupart Resides at Odanah, Wisconsin.

Chas. D. Armstrong Resides at Odanah, Wisconsin.

State of Wisconsin,

ss.

Ashland County,

BE IT REMEMBERED, That on the **6"**[sic] day of **August**, A.D. 19**18**, at **Ashland, Wisconsin** in said County, pursuant to notice duly given, as required by law, at a **Special** Term of the County Court of said County, **Charles Armstrong, one of the** subscribing witness**es** to the last will and testament of **Edwin Green**, late,

1

of **the Village of Odanah** , in said County, deceased hereunto annexed **were** produced and duly sworn and examined.

And the proofs having been heard before said Court, and the Court having thereupon found that said Instrument was in all things duly executed as **his** last will and testament by the said **Edwin Green.**

Thereupon said instrument was by the order and decree of said Court duly allowed and admitted to probate, as and for the last will and testament of **Edwin Green,** deceased.

S E A L.

In Testimony Whereof, I have hereunto set my hand and affixed the seal of the County Court of said County, at **Ashland, Wisconsin**, this **6"** day of **August** A. D. 19**18**.

Geo. H. McCloud   County Judge.

State of Wisconsin,)
               (ss.
Ashland County.   )

I, Jennie Johnson, Register in Probate in and for said Ashland County, do hereby certify that I have compared the within and foregoing copies with the original Will and Certificate of Probate, In the Matter of the Will of Edwin Green, deceased, now remaining on file and of record in this office, and that the same are true and correct copies of said original Will and Certificate of Probate, and of the whole thereof.

In Testimony Whereof, I have hereunto set my hand and affixed the seal of the County Court of said County, this 7th day of August, 1918.

Jennie Johnson
Register in Probate.

Probate
76520-18

Department of the Interior,
Office of Indian Affairs, Washington,
AUG 13, 1919
I have the honor to recommend that the certified copy of the will of Edwin Green be laid before the President for his approval.

Cate Sells
Commissioner

Department of The Interior
Office of The Secretary, Washington AUG 16 1919

I have the honor to recommend that the certified copy of the will of Edwin Green be approved.

Franklin K Payne
Secretary

The White House,
18 August 1919
Approved:

Woodrow Wilson

▲▼▲▼▲▼▲▼▲▼▲▼▲▼▲▼

GOOD DAY

WILL

I, **Good Day** of Pine Ridge Agency, South Dakota, Allottee number **518** do hereby make and declare this to be my last will and testament, in accordance with Section 2 of the Act of June 25, 1910, (36 stat. 855-858) and Act of February 14, 1913, (Public No. 381), hereby revoking all former wills made by me:

1. I hereby direct that as soon as possible after my decease, that all my debts, funeral and testamentary expenses be paid out of my personal estate.

2. I give and devise my allotment on the Pine Ridge Reservation, South Dakota, described as follows:

the W/2 of Section 25 in Twp. 40 north of Range 35 west of the Sixth Principal Meridian, South Dakota, containing 320 acres.

in the following manner:

To my cousin, Little Scout: all of my allotment.

3. I give and bequeath all of my personal property of whatsoever nature and wheresoever situated unto **in the following manner:**

3

To my grand-niece; Emma Kills-enemy-in-the-morning: one gray horse.

To Red Blanket: one black horse. Money I may have on deposit: to Little Scout, Red Blanket and Ada Shoulder, in equal shares.

4. All the rest of my property, real ~~or personal~~, now possessed or hereafter acquired, of whatsoever nature and wheresoever situated, I hereby give, devise and bequeath ~~unto~~ To Red Blanket and Ada Shoulder, in equal shares.

In witness whereof I have hereunto set my hand this 24th day of March 1915   FILED BY S. S. A.   *her mark*
                                        Good Day [thumb print]

The above statement was, this 24th day of March 1915 signed and published by Good Day as her last will and testament, in the joint presence of the undersigned, the said Good Day then being of sound and vigorous mind and free from any constraint or compulsion; whereupon we, being without any interest in the matter other than friendship, and being well acquainted with her but not members of her family, immediately subscribed our names hereto in the presence of each other and of the said testator, for the purpose of attesting the said will, as she requested us to do, her name being signed by George A. Trotter, one of the witnesses, at her request.

	Post Office Address
George A Trotter	Kyle, South Dakota.
Peter Chiefeagle	Kyle, South Dakota.

Pine Ridge, South Dakota.
October 22, 1918

I hereby certify that I have fully inquired into the mental competency of the Indian signing the above will; the circumstances attending the execution of the will; the influence that may have induced its execution, and the names of those entitled to share in the estate under the law of descent in South Dakota: reasons for the disposition of the property proposed by the will differing from disposition had the property descended by operation of law.

I respectfully forward this will with the recommendation that it be *dis*approved.

Henry M Tidwell
Supt. & Spl. Disb. Agent.

Department of The Interior,
Office of Indian Affairs, Washington,
JUN 27 1919

The within will of Good Day is hereby recommended for approval in accordance with the provisions of the Act of June 25, 1910 (36 Stats. L., 855-6) as amended by Act of February 14, 1913 (37 Stats. L., 678).

Respectfully,
EB Meritt
Assistant Commissioner

Department of The Interior
Office of The Secretary SEP 18 1919

The within will is hereby approved in accordance with the Act of June 25, 1910 (36 Stats. L., 855-6) as amended by Act of February 14, 1913 (37 Stats. L., 678).

SG Hopkins
Assistant Secretary

▲▼▲▼▲▼▲▼▲▼▲▼▲▼

MARY DECORY or LITTLE WILLOW

I Mary Decory being of sound and dividing mind and in consideration of the brevity of live I hereby make this my last will and testament revoking all wills heretofore by me made.

1ˢᵗ After all my just debts, funeral expenses and a proper monument erected on my grave have been paid out of my estate, I give and bequeath to my beloved son John Decory my house and lot located in Missiua[sic], South Dakota.

2ⁿᵈ In as much that my beloved daughters Julia Lacket, Mary Green and Nellie Presho being financially provided for I give and bequeath to each of them namely Julia Lacket, Mary Green, Nellie Presho five dollars to be paid out of my estate.

3ʳᵈ I give and bequeath to my beloved son John Decory six hundred ($600) to be paid out of my estate.

4th The balance of my estate I give and bequeath to my beloved children Giorga Decory, Benjamin Decory, Rose Edwards and my beloved grandchild Ethel Marion Edwards in equal shares to share alike.

I hereby appoint Claude J Anderson to be the executor and custodian of my last will and testament.

Signed by the said testator in our presence and at her request.

This twenty first day of November in the year of Our Lord 1917.

Witnesses to mark   *her*
C J Anderson   *Mary Decory*
Geo Rogers   *mark*

Probate
102334-18
 MHW

Department of the Interior,
Office of Indian Affairs, Washington,
Disapproval of will, Mary   SEP 26 1919
Decory, Rosebud, South Dak.

In accordance with the provisions of the Act of June 25, 1910 (36 Stat. L. 855-6) as amended by the Act of February 14, 1913 (37 Stat. L. 678) and the regulations of the Department, the within will of Mary Decory or Little Willow, deceased Rosebud Sioux allottee No. 7 1/2, is hereby recommended for disapproval in so far as her United States trust property is concerned.

                                     EB Merritt
                                     Assistant Commissioner

Department of The Interior
Office of The Secretary, Washington   AUG 31 1916

Pursuant to the provisions of the Act of June 25, 1910 (36 Stat. L. 855-6) as amended by the Act of February 14, 1913 (37 Stat. L. 678) and the regulations of the Department, the within will of Mary Decory or Little Willow, deceased Rosebud Sioux allottee No. 7 1/2, is hereby recommended for disapproval in so far as her United States trust property is concerned. No executor will be recognized.

3-27-AMG

SG Hopkins
Assistant Secretary

OFFICE OF INDIAN AFFAIRS
RECEIVED
SEP 19 1918
14781

OFFICE OF INDIAN AFFAIRS
RECEIVED
AUG 23 1919
72618

DAVID LEE

BE IT REMEMBERED THAT I, David Lee, Cheyenne River Sioux allottee No. 397, aged sixty-two years, being of sound and disposing mind and memory and wishing to make a final disposition of my allotment and other property, do hereby make, publish and declare this as and for my last will and testament, hereby revoking all other wills or codicils heretofore by me made.

First, to my beloved son Samuel Lee, who is living with and caring for me in my old age, I give, devise and bequeath that part of my allotment described as the S/2 of N/2 of Section 4 and Lots 1, 2, 3 and 4 of Section 4, Township 13 N., Range 28 E., B.H.M., S. D., containing approximately 320 acres, together with all improvements thereon.

Second, to my beloved son Henry lee, I give, devise and bequeath the remainder of my allotment, described as SW/4 of Section 4, Township 13 N., Range 28 E.; SW/4 of SW/4 of Section 23, Township 16 N., Range 28 E.; and S/2 of SE/4 and NW/4 of SE/4 of Section 32, Township 14 N., Range 28 E., B.H.M., S. D., containing approximately 320 acres.

Third, to my beloved sons Samuel and Henry Lee, I give, devise and bequeath all the rest of the property, real and personal, of which I may die possessed, in equal shares.

IN TESTIMONY WHEREOF I have hereunto set my hand and seal this *5* day of January, 1918, at LaPlant, South Dakota, in the presence of the attesting witnesses who have subscribed their names below.

(Seal)

David Lee
Testator.

SIGNED, SEALED, PUBLISHED AND DECLARED by the said David Lee, on the date first above mentioned, as and for his last will and testament, and at his request and in his presence and in the presence of each other we have hereunto subscribed our names as attesting witnesses.

Thomas G Smith   *Lucy P Smith*
La Plant, S. D.   *La Plant, So Dak.*

Department of The Interior,
Office of Indian Affairs, Washington,

OCT 8 1919

14781-1918
55916-1919

It is recommended that the within will be approved pursuant to the provisions of the Act of June 25, 1910 (36 Stats. L., 855-6) as amended by Act of February 14, 1913 (37 Stats. L., 678).

Respectfully,
EB Meritt
Assistant Commissioner

Department of The Interior
Office of The Secretary

The within will is hereby approved pursuant to the provisions of the Act of June 25, 1910 (36 Stats. L., 855-6) as amended by Act of February 14, 1913 (37 Stats. L., 678).

SG Hopkins
Assistant Secretary

▲▼▲▼▲▼▲▼▲▼▲▼▲▼

CHIEF EAGLE

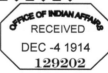

Original
WILL

OFFICE OF INDIAN AFFAIRS
RECEIVED
DEC -4 1914
129202

    I, **Chief Eagle** of Pine Ridge Agency, South Dakota, Allottee number **6853** do hereby make and declare this to be my last will and testament, in accordance with Section 2 of the Act of June 25, 1910, (36 stat. 855-858) and Act of February 14, 1913, (Public No. 381), hereby revoking all former wills made by me:

1. I hereby direct that as soon as possible after my decease, that all my debts, funeral and testamentary expenses be paid out of my personal

estate.

2. I give and devise my allotment on the Pine Ridge Reservation, South Dakota, described as follows:

The N/2 of Sec. 20 in Twp. 39 N. of Range 41 west of the 6th P.M. South Dakota, containing 320 acres.

in the following manner:

To my wife, Angelina Chief Eagle: the N/2 of NE/4 of Sec. 20 in Twp. 39 N. of Range 41 west of the 6th P.M.

To my son, Otto Chief Eagle: the S/2 of NE/4 of Sec. 20 in Twp. 39 N. of Range 41 west of the 6th P.M.

To my son, Peter Chief Eagle: the NW/4 of Sec. 20 in Twp. 39 N. of Range 41 west of the 6th P.M.

3. I give and bequeath all of my personal property of whatsoever nature and wheresoever situated unto

To my wife, Angelina Chief Eagle and my sons, Otto and Peter Chief Eagle, in equal shares.

4. All the rest of my property, real ~~or personal~~, now possessed or hereafter acquired, of whatsoever nature and wheresoever situated, I hereby give, devise and bequeath unto

my wife, Angelina Chief Eagle and my sons, Otto and Peter Chief Eagle, in equal shares.

In witness whereof I have hereunto set my hand this **23rd** day of **November** 1914.   *his* [thumb
                                                                            mark print]
                                                              Chief Eagle

The above statement was, this **23rd** day of **November** 1914, signed and published by **Chief Eagle** as **his** last will and testament, in the joint presence of the undersigned, the said **Chief Eagle** then being of sound and vigorous mind and free from any constraint or compulsion;

whereupon we, being without any interest in the matter other than friendship, and being well acquainted with **him** but not members of **his** family, immediately subscribed our names hereto in the presence of each other and of the said testator, for the purpose of attesting the said will, as **he** requested us to do, **his name being signed by George A Trotter, one of the witnesses, at his request.**

	Post Office Address
George A Trotter	**Kyle, South Dakota.**
Peter Bull Bear	**Kyle, South Dakota.**

Pine Ridge, South Dakota.
NOV 30 1914

I hereby certify that I have fully inquired into the mental competency of the Indian signing the above will; the circumstances attending the execution of the will; the influence that may have induced its execution, and the names of those entitled to share in the estate under the law of descent in South Dakota: reasons for the disposition of the property proposed by the will differing from disposition had the property descended by operation of law.

I respectfully forward this will with the recommendation that it be …..approved.

John R Brennan
Supt. & Spl. Disb. Agent.

Department of The Interior,
Office of Indian Affairs, Washington,
DEC 22 1914

The within will of Chief Eagle is recommended for approval in accordance with the provisions of the Act of June 25, 1910 (36 Stats. L., 855-6) as amended by Act of February 14, 1913 (37 Stats. L., 678).

EB Meritt
Assistant Commissioner

Department of The Interior
Office of The Secretary DEC 22 1914

The within will of Chief Eagle is approved in accordance with the Act of June 25, 1910 (36 Stats. L., 855-6) as amended by Act of February 14, 1913 (37 Stats. L., 678).

Bo Sweeney
Assistant Secretary

▲ ▼▲ ▼▲ ▼▲ ▼▲ ▼▲ ▼▲ ▼▲ ▼

AH WAY

31180-1919

I, Ah way Comanche, Fam. #588 1/4, of Apache, Okla., do hereby make and publish my last will and testament.

I give, and bequeath to my husband John Chibitty, the sum of one dollar, disinheriting him from the rest of my property, both personal and real, for the reason that he has failed to support and care for me during my sickness.

I give, devise and bequeath to my children Pansy Sapcut, Frank Sapcut, George Sapcut, Page Too ah nip ah and Esther Parker all the rest and residue of my estate; real or personal encluding[sic] my allotment the N^2 of SE^4 of Sec. 27 Twp 59 Rge. 11 W I.M., to be divided among them in equal portions.

her

Ahway [thumb print]

mark

Signed, published and declared by the above named Ahway, as and for her last will and testament in presence of us, who in his & her presence and in the presence of each other and at her request have hereunto subscribed our names as witnesses.

Victoria Weryaclswe

P W Lotham

I hereby certify that I speak both the English & Comanche language and that the above will is correct a to the wishes of Ahway.

Lizzie Watch mam sook wat

Interpreter.

Department of The Interior,   SEP 19 1919
Office of Indian Affairs, Washington,

It is recommended that the within will of Ah-way be approved under the Act of June 25, 1910 (36 Stats. L., 855-6) as amended by Act of February 14, 1913 (37 Stats. L., 678), and the regulations of the Department.

Respectfully,

EB Meritt

Assistant Commissioner

Department of The Interior OCT -6 1919
Office of The Secretary

The within will of Ah-way, deceased, is hereby approved under the Act of June 25, 1910 (36 Stats. L., 855-6) as amended by Act of February 14, 1913 (37 Stats. L., 678), and the regulations of the Department.

SG Hopkins
Assistant Secretary

▲▼▲▼▲▼▲▼▲▼▲▼▲▼▲▼

CHARLES ELK

In the Name of God, Amen

I, **Charles Elk**   of **Bristow**   in the County of **Boyd**   and State of **Nebraska**, *being of sound mind and memory, and considering the uncertainty of this frail and transitory life, do therefore make, ordain, publish and declare this to be my last* Will and Testament:

FIRST, *I order and direct that my Executor   hereinafter named, pay all my just debts and funeral expenses as soon after my decease as conveniently may be.*

SECOND, *After the payment of such funeral expenses and debts, I give, devise and bequeath*

To my wife, Myrtle Lillian Elk all my interest in lands of which I may die siezed[sic] also all money and other property of whatsoever nature.

It is also my desire and wish that my son Howard Elk be given the proper care and schooling and be brought up in the nurture and admonition of the Lord.

The support medical attention and all expenses for the keeping of my son Howard to be paid out of the proceeds of my estate.

LASTLY, *I make, constitute and appoint* **Thomas O Knudson** *to be Executor   of this, my last Will and Testament, hereby revoking all former Wills by me made.*

IN WITNESS WHEREOF, I have hereunto subscribed my name and affixed my seal the **4th** *day of* **March** *in the year of our Lord, one thousand nine hundred* **Eighteen** *.*

Charles Elk   Seal

This Instrument was, on the day of the date thereof, signed, published and declared by said testator **Charles Elk** *to be his last Will and Testament, in our presence, who, at* **his** *request, have subscribed our names hereto as witnesses, in* **his** *presence, and in the presence of each other.*

Frank Talich

L A Van Horn

Department of The Interior,
Office of Indian Affairs, Washington,
SEP 28 1919

The within will of Charles Elk is hereby recommended for disapproval in accordance with the Act of June 25, 1910 (36 Stats. L., 855-6) as amended by Act of February 14, 1913 (37 Stats. L., 678).

Respectfully,

EB Meritt

Assistant Commissioner

Department of The Interior
Office of The Secretary OCT -6 1919

The within will is hereby disapproved in accordance with the Act of June 25, 1910 (36 Stats. L., 855-6) as amended by Act of February 14, 1913 (37 Stats. L., 678).

SG Hopkins

Assistant Secretary

▲▼▲▼▲▼▲▼▲▼▲▼▲▼▲▼

CATHERINE MITCHELL

LAST WILL AND TESTAMENT
of
CATHERINE MITCHELL.

I, Catherine Mitchell, of Tacoma, Pierce County, Wash., being of

13

sound and disposing mind and memory, do hereby make, publish and declare this to be my last will and testament, hereby revoking and all former wills by me at any time heretofore made.

FIRST: It is my desire that my executor, herein after named shall as soon as he has sufficient funds in his hands, pay all just charges for administration and funeral expenses.

SECOND: I hereby devise and bequeath to each of my children who survive me, the following, to-wit: To Lillie Tittle, I give my silver set, also my upholstered parlor set; to Lizzie LeClaire, I give my silver knives and forks; to Emily Hunt, I give the picture of her father, Theo. Gard; to Nettie Varner, I give my own picture and the picture of my mother; and to Laura Varner, I give my moon stone earrings.

THIRD: To Nellie Perkins, I give and bequeath my watch and chain and my sewing machine.

FOURTH: I direct that all interest I have in Lots Eight (8), eleven (11) and twelve (12), in Block Eight Thousand Three Hundred Fifty-seven (8357) in the Indian Addition to the City of Tacoma, shall be sold by my executor hereinafter named, as soon as he can obtain a price therefor[sic] which in his judgment is fair and reasonable, and convert the same into cash; that from the proceeds of said sale, the expenses of my last sickness and funeral shall be paid, and if there be any surplus remaining that such surplus money be equally divided amongst all of my daughters who survive me.

FIFTH: My allotment on the Yakima Reservation, Wash., I give, devise and bequeath to my husband, John Mitchell, my daughters, Laura Varner; Nettie Varner; Emily Hunt; Lizzie LeClaire and Lillie Tittle, and to Nellie Perkins, or to such of them as survive me, in equal shares.

SIXTH: Any and all other estate of which I die seized or have any interest in, I give, devise and bequeath to my husband John Mitchell.

SEVENTH: Should my husband, John Mitchell, die before my own death, then and in that event, I give, devise and bequeath to my daughters who survive me and to Nellie Perkins, share and share alike, all my estate of which I may die seized or have any interest in whatsoever.

14

EIGHTH: I hereby constitute and appoint my said husband, John Mitchell, the executor of this my last will and testament, and I hereby give to him full power to grant, bargain, sell and convey any and all of my property and estate, whether it be real, personal or mixed, and empower him to take possession and control thereof; and I further direct that no bond be required of him as executor of this will; and that after the proving of this will, he shall settle my said estate without the intervention of any court.

In Witness Whereof, I hereunto set my hand and seal this *12* day of January, A.D., 1913.

her
Catherine X Mitchell
mark

The foregoing writing was signed, sealed, published and declared by the above named Catherine Mitchell as and for her last will and testament, in the presence of us, who at her request and in her presence and in the presence of each other, have subscribed our names as attesting witnesses thereto this *12* day of January, A.D., 1913.

> *Ida McQuesten*
> Residing at Tacoma, Washington.
> *G Down McQuesten*
> Residing at Tacoma, Washington.

I certify that I signed the testator's name in her presence and at her request, -she signing by "x mark"

> *G Down McQuesten*

Department of The Interior,
Office of Indian Affairs, Washington,
JUL 9 1919

The foregoing will of Catherine Mitchell, Yakima allottee No. 3965, so far as it applies to her trust property is recommended for approval in accordance with the Act of June 25, 1910 (36 Stats. L., 855-6) as amended by Act of February 14, 1913 (37 Stats. L., 678).

> Respectfully,
> *EB Meritt*
> Assistant Commissioner

Department of The Interior
Office of The Secretary   JUL 15 1919

The foregoing will of Catherine Mitchell, Yakima allottee 3965, so far as it applies to her trust property is hereby approved in accordance with the Act of June 25, 1910 (36 Stats. L., 855-6) as amended by Act of February 14, 1913 (37 Stats. L., 678).

SG Hopkins
Assistant Secretary

▲▼▲▼▲▼▲▼▲▼▲▼▲▼▲

SAMUEL MEDICINE BULL

Last Will and Testament
of
Samuel Medicine Bull

OFFICE OF INDIAN AFFAIRS
RECEIVED
OCT 27 1916
112149

In the Name of God, Amen,

I, Samuel Medicine Bull of the Lower Brule Reservation, South Dakota, being of sound mind, memory and understanding do hereby make and publish this my last will and testament, hereby revoking and annulling all wills heretofore made in manner and form following, that is to say:

First, I direct that all my just debts and funeral expenses of my last illness shall be paid by my executor, hereinafter named as soon after my decease as shall be convenient.

Second, all the rest and residue of my estate both real and personal and mixed, I give, devise, and bequath[sic] to my wife, Mary Medicine Bull 160 acres (One hundred and sixty) also the house and other improvements thereon, which is now a part of my allotment, with the provision that my daughter, Annie Medicine Bull, shall have the privilege of living in the house as long as she so desires. I also devise, bequath[sic] and give to my daughter, Annie Medicine Bull the balance of my allotment which contains a fraction over 160 acres. Further I give devise and bequath[sic] to my daughter, Annie Medicine Bull, 1 gray mare and colt branded (Note: Symbol was curved line ⌐ over the letter S) on right hip, and to my wife, Mary Medicine Bull, one black gelding branded (Note: Same symbol as above) on right hip, and one

16

white mare branded (Note: Same symbol as above) on right hip. Further I give devise and bequeath 16 head of horses, mares and colts branded (Note: Same symbol as above) on right hop to my daughter, Annie Medicine Bull, and 15 head of horses mares and colts to my wife, Mary Medicine Bull. It being understood that the division shall be supervised by the Superintendent of livestock at the Lower Brule Agency, SD.

Further, I give devise and bequeath to my wife, Mary Medicine Bull, one-half of the funds deposited to my credit under the jurisdiction of the Superintendent of the Lower Brule Agency, and the remaining one-half to my daughter, Annie Medicine Bull.

And lastly, I do hereby nominate, constitute and appoint Rev. Luke C. Walker executor of this my last Will and Testament.

In Testimony whereof, I have set my hand and seal to this my last Will and Testament, at Lower Brule, South Dakota, this 17th day of October, 1916.

Samuel Medicine Bull

Signed, Sealed, Published and Declared by the said Samuel Medicine Bull in our presence as and for his last Will and Testament and at his request and in his presence and in the presence of each other, we have hereunto subscribed our names as attesting witnesses thereto.

Hiram N. Clark
Lower Brule, SD.
Rev. Luke C Walker
Lower Brule, SD
K K Karean
Lower Brule, SD

Probate
78803-18
 L A P

Department of The Interior,
Office of Indian Affairs, Washington,
JUN 27 1919

The within will dated October 17, 1916, of Samuel Medicine Bull, deceased Lower Brule Sioux allottee No. 376, is hereby recommended for

17

approval in accordance with the Act of June 25, 1910 (36 Stats. L., 855-6) as amended by Act of February 14, 1913 (37 Stats. L., 678).

Respectfully,
EB Meritt
Assistant Commissioner

Department of The Interior
Office of The Secretary JUL 15 1919

The within will dated October 17, 1916, of Samuel Medicine Bull, deceased Lower Brule Sioux allottee No. 376, is hereby recommended for approval in accordance with the Act of June 25, 1910 (36 Stats. L., 855-6) as amended by Act of February 14, 1913 (37 Stats. L., 678).

SG Hopkins
Assistant Secretary

FOLLOWS HER

OFFICE OF INDIAN AFFAIRS
RECEIVED
OCT 21 1919
90254

OFFICE OF INDIAN AFFAIRS
RECEIVED
DEC 22 1918
150415

Crow Creek Allottee No. 602.

LAST WILL AND TESTAMENT OF FOLLOWS HER.

IN THE NAME OF GOD, AMEN.

I, Follows Her, of Crow Creek Indian Reservation, Crow Creek, Buffalo County, South Dakota, being of sound mind, memory and understanding, do hereby make and publish this my last will and testament, hereby revoking and annulling all wills by me heretofore made, in manner and form following, that is to say:

FIRST. I direct that all my just debts and funeral expenses, and expenses of my last illness shall be paid by my executor hereinafter names, as soon after my decease as shall be convenient.

SECOND. I have an allotment of land of my own within the Crow Creek Indian Reservation, South Dakota, described as the North half and the Southeast quarter of the Northeast quarter and the Lot 3 of Section 19, and the Northwest quarter of Section 20, all in Township 108 North of Range 75 West of the Fifth Principal Meridian. I have some money in bank under the supervision of the Superintendent of the Crow Creek Indian School, and I have made application for my share of the Tribal Trust Fund due me as a member of the Crow Creek or Lower Yanktonai Sioux Indians. All of my lands herein described, and all of my moneys herein mentioned, including the money due me from the Tribal Trust Fund, I hereby give, devise and bequeath to my daughters, Good Road Woman of Standing Rock Reservation and Mrs. Medicine Cedar of Crow Creek Agency, each of my said daughters to have and take an undivided One-half interest in my lands and each to have and take one-half of all of my moneys of every character. I have one cow and one calf and I give and bequeath them to my daughter Mrs. Medicine Cedar.

I have only two living children and they are my daughters Good Road Woman and Mrs. Medicine Cedar herein above named by me. I give my lands and property to them as I have herein stated because they care for and look after and support me. I have several grandchildren but they do not care for me nor help me nor come about me and I do not give them any of my property for those reasons. I am a widow and now live with my daughter Mrs. Medicine Cedar.

AND LASTLY, I do hereby nominate, constitute and appoint my daughter Mrs. Medicine Cedar as executor of this my last will and testament.

IN TESTIMONY WHEREOF, I have set my hand and seal to this, my last will and testament, at Crow Creek Agency, Crow Creek, South Dakota, this 13th day of December, in the year of our Lord 1913.

her
FOLLOWS HER; [thumb print]
mark

Signed, sealed, published and declared by the said Follows Her in our presence as and for her last will and testament, and at her request and in her presence, and in the presence of each other, we have hereunto subscribed our names as attesting witnesses thereto.

Homer J Bibb	Crow Creek, S.D.
Alice H Denomie	Crow Creek, S.D.
John Saul	Crow Creek, S.D.

Department of The Interior,
Office of Indian Affairs, Washington,

It is recommended that the will be approved, pursuant to the provisions of the Act of June 25, 1910 (36 Stats. L., 855-6) as amended by Act of February 14, 1913 (37 Stats. L., 678).

Respectfully,
EB Meritt
Assistant Commissioner

Department of The Interior
Office of The Secretary   JAN 16 1915

The within will is approved pursuant to the provisions of the Act of June 25, 1910 (36 Stats. L., 855-6) as amended by Act of February 14, 1913 (37 Stats. L., 678).

Bo Sweeney
Assistant Secretary

▲▼▲▼▲▼▲▼▲▼▲▼▲▼▲▼

EMMA SHANE nee ONE STAR or WHITE WOMAN

Last Will and Testament

of   FILED BY C. P. F.

Emma Shane nee One Star

IN THE NAME OF GOD, AMEN.

I, *Emma Shane nee One Star* of *Crow Indian Tribe* being of sound mind, memory, and understanding, do hereby make and publish this my last will and testament, hereby revoking and annulling all wills by me heretofore made, in manner and form following, that is to say:

First; I direct that all my just debts and funeral expenses, and expenses of my last illness shall be paid by my executor hereinafter named as soon after my decease as convenient;

Second; I give, devise and bequeath to

My Grand daughter Amy Yellow Tail nee Medicine Crow the following

described land; SE1/4 of the NE1/4, Sec 35 Twp. 6 S.R. 35 E

One Star, My husband and his mother, to have the privilege of living with Amy Yellow Tail nee Medicine Crow on this tract of land..

Third; All the rest and residue of my estate, both real, and personal and mixed, I give devise and bequeath to my lawful heirs as determined after my decease.

And lastly; I do hereby nominate, constitute and appoint **Evan W. Estep** executor of this my last will and testament.

In testimony Whereof, I have set my hand and seal to this, my last will and Testament, at **Lodge Grass** Montana, this **13** day of **July**, in the year of our Lord one thousand nine hundred and **15**.

her
Emma Shane nee One Star [thumb print]
mark.

Signed, sealed, published and declared by said **Emma Shane nee One Star** in our presence, as and for **the** last Will and testament, and at **her** request and in our presence, and in the presence of each other, we have hereunto subscribed our names as attesting witnesses thereto.

John F Hargrave	of		
(Signature Illegible)	of		*his*
Interpreter.	of	*Scolds the Bear*	[thumb print]
		Crow Indian Policeman	*mark*

Probate
37091- 18
61985- 19
 M H W

Approved will of Emma Shane One
Stat[sic] or White Woman, deceased Crow
allottee No. 850.

Department of The Interior,
Office of Indian Affairs, Washington,
                    OCT 23 1919

The within will of Emma Shane One Stat[sic] or White Woman, deceased Crow allottee No. 850, is hereby recommended for approval in accordance with the provisions of the Act of June 25, 1910 (36 Stats. L., 855-6) as amended by Act of February 14, 1913 (37 Stats. L., 678).

EB Meritt
Assistant Commissioner

Department of The Interior
Office of The Secretary OCT 25 1919

Pursuant to the provisions of the Act of June 25, 1910 (36 Stats. L., 855-6) as amended by Act of February 14, 1913 (37 Stats. L., 678) and the Regulations of the Department, I hereby approve the within will of Emma Shane One Star or White Woman, deceased Crow allottee No. 850.

SG Hopkins
Assistant Secretary

OFFICE OF INDIAN AFFAIRS
RECEIVED
SEP 25 1919
83243

RUTH TYLER BOSIN

TO ALL TO WHOM THESE PRESENTS MAY COME, GREETING; I, Ruth Ryler[sic] Bosin, realizing the uncertainty of life and the uncertainty[sic] of death, being now of sound and disposing mind, and desiring to dispose of my property and business affairs hereby make, publish and declare this my last Will and Testament, revoking any and all Will and Cidicils[sic] heretofore made.

I give and bequeath to my son, John Bosin, Jr., South Half (1/2) of North-west Quarter (1/4) of Section Thirteen (13), Township Thirteen (13) North of Range Nine (9) West if Indian Meridian.

I also give and bequeath to my great-aunt, Sage Woman Tyler, my undivided one-fourth (1/4) interest in the allotment of Mrs. Black Kettle, deceased Cheyenne allottee No. 2031, described as the E/2 of SE/4 of Sec. 29, T. 16 N., R. 12, W. I.M.

I give and bequeath to my husband, John Bosin, my Oldsmobile automobile.

I give and bequeath to my son, John Bosin, Jr., all the remainder and residue of any and all property, both real and personal, of which I may die possessed.

I further direct that in case of my death the paternal grand-mother of my son, John Bosin, Jr., shall have his care and custody until such time as his father, John Bosin, may be in position to assume such care and custody.

It is my wish that the Superintendent of the Kiowa and Comanche Indian Agency at Anadarko, Oklahoma, and his sucessors[sic] in office, immediately upon my death take charge of and assume the care and custody of any and all property, both real and personal, descending to my son John Bosin, Jr., in accordance with the terms of this Will.

I further direct that any and all debts, funeral expenses etc., be paid from any moneys to my credit in the office of the Cheyenne & Arapaho Agency, at Concho, Oklahoma.

Ruth Tyler Bosin.

We, the undersigned, witnesses to the above Will, hereby certify that same was written as stated by the testator and was signed by her in our presence and in the presence of each other on this the 17th day of December, 1917.

E. M. Goss
M. C. McCafferty
C. C. Thompson.

In explanation of the apparent disinheritance of my husband, John Bosin, in my will this day executed, I give as my reason for leaving to my son, John Bosin, Jr., my entire estate other than the automobile mentioned the fact that my said husband has a valuable allotment in his own name while our son, John Bosin, Jr., has nothing other than the property here bequeathed to him and further that it is my intention to give him such an amount from funds in my possession as will fully equalize the distribution herein made.

Ruth Tyler Bosin.

Witnesses:

E. M. Goss
M. C. McCafferty
C. C. Thompson.

I hereby certify on honor that the above and foregoing is a true, correct and exact copy of the original will made by Ruth Tyler Bosin on Dec. 17, 1917.

W.W. Scott,
Supt. and Spl. Disb. Agent.

Cheyenne & Arapaho Agency
Concho, Okla. Jan. 8, 1918.

Department of The Interior,
Office of Indian Affairs, Washington,

OCT 20 1919

It is recommended that the within will of Ruth Tyler Bosin be approved under the Act of June 25, 1910 (36 Stats. L., 855-6) as amended by Act of February 14, 1913 (37 Stats. L., 678), so far as the same relates to her trust property.

Respectfully,
EB Meritt
Assistant Commissioner

10 FL 14

Department of The Interior
Office of The Secretary   OCT 31 1919

The within will of Ruth Tyler Bosin, deceased, is hereby approved under the Act of June 25, 1910 (36 Stats. L., 855-6) as amended by Act of February 14, 1913 (37 Stats. L., 678), so far as the same relates to her trust property.

SG Hopkins
Assistant Secretary

▲▼▲▼▲▼▲▼▲▼▲▼▲▼▲▼

MARY PUNCH TUCKER

LAST WILL AND TESTAMENT OF MARY PUNCH TUCKER.

In the Name Of God, Amen: I, Mary Punch Tucker, of White Oak, Okla., being of sound and disposing mind, a member of the Eastern Shawnee tribe of Indians, thirty-three years of age, and ever remembering the certainty of death and the uncertainty of the time thereof, do hereby make, publish and declare this to be my last will and testament, in manner and form as follows:

I hereby give, will and devise the North Half of Southwest Quarter of Southeast Quarter of Section Two in Township Twenty-seven North of Range Twenty-four East of the Indian Meridian, situate[sic] in Ottawa County, State of Oklahoma, to my beloved daughter, Ruth May Tucker.

In testimony whereof I have hereunto set my hand and seal this third day of July in the year of Our Lord One Thousand Nine Hundred and Eighteen.

Her

Mary Punch Tucker [thumb print]

mark.

Signed, sealed, published and declared by Mary Punch Tucker, the above named testatrix in the presence of us, who at her request, in her presence, and in the presence of each other, have hereunto set our names, as subscribing and attesting witnesses to the foregoing instrument as the last will and testament of the said Mary Punch Tucker on this the third day of July in the Year of Our Lord One Thousand Nine Hundred and Eighteen.

P.O. Address	*Wyandotte, Okla.*	Signature	*C.E. Lewis*
P.O. ADDRESS	*Wyandotte, Okla.*	Signature	*RB Demarce*

I hereby certify that Mary Punch Tucker speaks and understands the English language well although she does not write and that the above instrument was made at her request, in accordance with her expressed wishes and was read to her by me before she signed it.

Carl F Mayer

Supt.

PROBATE
9524-19
 L L

Department of The Interior,
Office of Indian Affairs, Washington, OCT 24 1919

It is recommended that the within will be approved pursuant to the provisions of the Act of June 25, 1910 (36 Stats. L., 855-6) as amended by Act of February 14, 1913 (37 Stats. L., 678).

Respectfully,

EB Meritt

Assistant Commissioner

Department of The Interior

Office of The Secretary OCT 28 1919

The within will is hereby approved pursuant to the provisions of the Act of June 25, 1910 (36 Stats. L., 855-6) as amended by Act of February 14, 1913 (37 Stats. L., 678).

SG Hopkins

Assistant Secretary

▲ ▼ ▲ ▼ ▲ ▼ ▲ ▼ ▲ ▼ ▲ ▼ ▲ ▼

OFFICE OF INDIAN AFFAIRS OF INDIANA

RECEIVED

OCT 17 1919

89087   66335

KILLED MANY

LAST WILL AND TESTAMENT OF

KILLED MANY.

IN THE NAME OF GOD, AMEN.

I, Killed Many, of the Crow Creek Reservation in South Dakota, being of sound mind, memory and understanding, do hereby make and publish this my last will and Testament, hereby revoking and annulling all wills by me heretofore made, in manner and form following, that is to say:

FIRST, I direct that all my just debts and funeral expenses, and expenses of my last illness shall be paid by my executor hereinafter named as soon after my decease as shall be convenient;

SECOND, I give, devise and bequeath my allotment of land described as the South half of the North half and the North half of the South half of section thirteen (13), township one-hundred six (106) Range seventy-one (71) consisting of three hundred twenty acres (320 A.) to the following names persons, each to take the part herein described, as follows: To Whisper, my beloved wife, I give the South half of the North west quarter of Section 13, township 106, Range 71, consisting of 80 acres. To Susan Tuttle, my step-daughter, I give the North half of the South half of Section 13, Township 106, Range 71, consisting of 160 acres. I give her this part of my real estate for the reason that she received no allotment of her own and I raised her the same as if she were my own daughter. To Hattie Cook, m daughter, I give the South west quarter of the North East quarter of section 13, Township 106, Range 71, consisting of 40 acres. To Shaker Woman, of Standing Rock Reservation, my niece, I give the Southeast quarter of the North east quarter of section 13, Township 106, Range 71, consisting of 40 acres,

THIRD, I give and bequeath one of my mares to my wife, Whisper, and the other to my daughter, Hattie Cook; I have only two mares.

FOURTH, All the rest and residue of my estate, both real and personal, I give, devise and bequeath to my wife, Whisper.

My wife is named Whisper. Hattie Cook above named is my only living daughter. All of my other children are dead. I had only three children in all; one of these if Hattie Cook, heretofore named; another was Mary Killed Many who died at Hampton Institute when she was about 19 years of age, unmarried and without issue; the other was also named Mary Killed Many and she grew up to womanhood, was married and left five children at the time of her death about six years ago, all of whom are now living. The names of these children are, Mabel Stricker, David Stricker, Clara Stricker, Louis Stricker and Lorena Stricker, all living at Greenwood, South Dakota. These five children of Mary Killed Many, deceased are the only grand-children I have, and I give them nothing for the reason that their father is able to care for them.

AND LASTLY, I do hereby nominate, constitute and appoint Thomas W. Tuttle, executor of this my last Will and Testament.

IN WITNESS WHEREOF, I have set my hand and seal to this, my last Will and Testament, at the Crow Creek Agency Office, on the Crow Creek Reservation, in South Dakota, this 17th day of May, in the year of our Lord, One thousand, nine hundred and thirteen.

KILLED MANY, His Mark: [thumb print]

SIGNED, SEALED, PUBLISHED AND DECLARED by the said Killed Many, in our presence, as and for his last Will and Testament, and at his request and in our presence, and in the presence of each other, we have hereunto subscribed our names as attesting witnesses thereto.

(Signature Illegible)	Residence, Crow Creek, So. Dakota.
Rosa Little Bird	Residence, Crow Creek, So. Dakota.
Thomas W Tuttle	Residence, Crow Creek, So. Dakota.

Department of The Interior,
Office of Indian Affairs, Washington, JUN 24 1913

It is recommended that the within will be approved pursuant to the provisions of the Act of February 14, 1913 (Public 381).

CF Hawke
2 Asst. ~~Acting~~ Commissioner

Department of The Interior JUN 24 1913
Office of The Secretary

Within will approved pursuant to the provisions of the Act of February 14, 1913 (Public 381).

Suirus Saylin
Assistant Secretary

▲▼▲▼▲▼▲▼▲▼▲▼▲▼

WAH-KO (WALK-KO)

LAST WILL AND TESTAMENT OF Wah-ko (Walk-ko);

KNOW ALL MEN BY THESE PRESENTS: That I Wah-ko (Walk-ko) a Sac and Fox Indian, of Kickapoo Reservation, Brown County, Kansas being seventy three years of age and of sound mind and memory do hereby make, publish and declare this my last will and Testament hereby revoking and annuling[sic] any and all other last Wills and Testaments by me heretofore made.

First.

I desire all my just debts, expenses of last sickness and funeral expenses to be paid as soon after my decease as the same can conveniently be done.

Second.

I give, devise and bequeath to my beloved daughter, Blanche Spitto, age thirty six, all of Kickapoo allotment No. 87, Nah-kah-ti-e-sheck, described as E/2 of SW/4 Sec. 17, Twp. 4 S, Range 16 E. inherited by me (Land-Sales 105392-1911).

Third.

I give, devise and bequeath to my beloved son, Warren Wah-ko, age thirty seven, all of my interest in Kickapoo allotment No. 20, Mattow-o-sah, described as E/2 of NW/4, Sec. 30, Twp 4 S. Range 16 E. inherited land. (Las-Heirship 126976-12).

Fourth.

I give, devise, and bequeath to my two children, Blanche Spitto, and Warren Wah-ko, all of my personal property amounting to Eight thousand ($8000) Dollars, which is deposited with the Superintendent of Kickapoo Agency, to be divided equally between them share and share alike, after all my debts are paid.

IN TESTIMONY WHEREOF I have hereunto subscribed my name this 19th day of August, A.D. 1918 in the presence of Josephine D. Andres and Supt. L.S. Bonnin, whom I request to subscribe their names hereto as witnesses to the execution hereof.

his
Wah-ko (Walk-ko) [thumb print]
mark

I hereby solemnly swear that I have truthfully and correctly translated the above will from the English Language into the Kickapoo language to the best of my knowledge and ability.

Blanche Spitto
Interpreter

STATE OF KANSAS
            SS
BROWN COUNTY

We, the undersigned hereby certify that we saw the above names testator Wah-ko, subscribe his name to the foregoing instrument and heard him declare the same to be his last Will and Testament and that we at his request and in his presence and in the presence of each other subscribe our names hereto as witnesses to the execution hereof, this 19th day of August, A.D. 1918.

LS Bonnin, Supt
Josephine D Andres
Finan Clerk

~~Subscribed and sworn to before me this **19th** day of Aug. 1918.~~

~~*LS Bonnin*~~
~~Superintendent.~~

(The above crossed out on the microfilm.)

Department of The Interior,
Office of Indian Affairs, Washington, NOV 3 1919

It is recommended that the within will of Wah-ko or Walk-ko be approved under the Act of June 25, 1910 (36 Stats. L., 855-6) as amended by Act of February 14, 1913 (37 Stats. L., 678), and the regulations of the Department.

Respectfully,
EB Meritt
Assistant Commissioner

Department of The Interior NOV -5 1919
Office of The Secretary

The within will of Wah-ko or Walk-ko is hereby approved under the Act of June 25, 1910 (36 Stats. L., 855-6) as amended by Act of February 14, 1913 (37 Stats. L., 678), and the regulations of the Department.

SG Hopkins
Assistant Secretary

▲▼▲▼▲▼▲▼▲▼▲▼▲▼▲▼

WILLIAM HILL

Last Will of   DEPARTMENT OF THE INTERIOR
William Hill,
Allottee #488   UNITED STATES INDIAN SERVICE

Indian Wills, 1911 – 1921 Book Six
Records of The Bureau of Indian Affairs

Oneida, Wis., May 24, 1916.

State of Wisconsin,)
County of Brown.)

I, William Hill, of the Town of Hobart, County of Brown, State of Wisconsin, do make this my last will and testament:

I give, devise and bequeath my property, real and personal as follows:

To my daughter, Samantha S. King I give all my personal property and real estate, and especially one certain tract of land described as Claim No. 168 of T. 24 N. R. 19 E. of the 4th P.M. Wis., containing 15 acres.

In witness whereof I have signed, sealed, published and declared this instrument as my Will, at Oneida, Wisconsin, this 24th day of May, 1916.

his
William Hill mark [thumb print]

Witnesses to mark:
JC Hart
WB Horn

The said William Hill, at Oneida, Wisconsin, on the said 24th day of May, 1916, signed and sealed this instrument, and published and declared the same as and for his last will in our presence, and we, at his request, and in his presence and in the presence of each other, have hereunto written our names as subscribing witnesses.

JC Hart
WB Horn

Department of The Interior,
Office of Indian Affairs, Washington,
OCT 20 1919

The within will of William Hill is hereby recommended for approval in accordance with the Act of June 25, 1910 (36 Stats. L., 855-6) as amended by Act of February 14, 1913 (37 Stats. L., 678).

Respectfully,
EB Meritt
Assistant Commissioner

Department of The Interior
Office of The Secretary OCT 24 1919

The within will is hereby approved in accordance with the provisions of the Act of June 25, 1910 (36 Stats. L., 855-6) as amended by Act of February 14, 1913 (37 Stats. L., 678).

SG Hopkins
Assistant Secretary

▲▼▲▼▲▼▲▼▲▼▲▼▲▼
MRS. MARIE C. LENNARD SANDMANN or RENA HEATON

I, Mrs. Marie C. Lennard Sandmann, of the City of Yerington, County of Lyon, in the State of Nevada, being of sound and disposing mind, memory, and understanding, and considering the certainty of death, and the uncertainty of the time thereof, do therefore make, publish and declare this to be my last will and testament, in the manner following, that is to say:

1. I give devise and bequeath all my property, real, personal and mixed to my son Frederick B. Lennard and my daughter Jean Marie Lennard, share and share alike.

2. I hereby appoint T. E. Lennard and F. J. Lennard, or either of them that may be alive at the time of my death to be the executor or executors of this my last will and testament.

3. If either of my said children shall not have reached the age of twenty-one years at the time of my death, I hereby appoint my said executors, or either of them that may be alive at the time of my death to be the guardians of the person and estate of any minor child during minority.

IN WITNEWW WHEREOF, I, the said Marie C. Lennard Sandmann have hereunto set my hand this 16th day of February, A.D. one thousand nine hundred and fifteen.

Marie C. Lennard Sandmann   (seal)

The foregoing instrument, consisting of one page, was, t the date hereof, by the said Marie C. Lennard Sandman[sic] signed, sealed and published as, and declared to be, her last Will and Testament, in the presence of us, who, at her request, and in her presence, and in the presence of each other, have subscribed our names as witnesses hereto.

> E. H. Whitacre
> Residing at Yerington, Nevada
> H. Hanson
> Residing at Yerington, Nevada

State of Nevada, |
| *ss*
County of Lyon |

    I, CHAS. A. McLEOD, County Clerk and ex-officio Clerk of the **Eighth** Judicial District Court of the State of Nevada in and for Lyon County, said Court being a Court of Record, having common law jurisdiction, and a Clerk and a Seal, do hereby certify that the foregoing is a full, true and correct copy of the original **last will and testament of Marie C. Lennard Sandmann, deceased, which was duly admitted to probate by order of said Court duly given and made in that certain cause now therein pending, entitled "In The Matter of the Estate of Marie C. Lennard Sandmann, Deceased", and** which now remains on file and recorded in my office at Yerington, in said county.

In Testimony Whereof, I have hereunto set my hand and affixed the Seal of Said Court, at Yerington, this *13th* day of *June* A.D., 1917.

> *Chas A. McLeod*   Clerk
>   Deputy.

Probate
14306-18

Department of The Interior,
Office of Indian Affairs, Washington,

The within will of Marie C. Lennard Sandmann or Rena Heaton is hereby recommended for approval in accordance with the provisions of the Act of June 25, 1910 (36 Stats. L., 855-6) as amended by Act of February 14, 1913 (37 Stats. L., 678).

> *EB Meritt*
> Assistant Commissioner

Department of The Interior
Office of The Secretary NOV 11 1919

The within will is hereby approved in accordance with the provisions of the Act of June 25, 1910 (36 Stats. L., 855-6) as amended by Act of February 14, 1913 (37 Stats. L., 678).

SG Hopkins
Assistant Secretary

▲▼▲▼▲▼▲▼▲▼▲▼▲▼▲▼

MARGARET ENOS #1

Salt River Indian Agency,
Saltriver, Arizona, October 13, 1915.

I, Margaret Enos, a Pima Indian, being of sound mind and realizing the uncertainties of life and desiring to make certain provision for the future, do by these presents make known to all men that upon the event of my death I hereby bequeath and convey my property to the parties and in the parcels set forth herein.

To Alice Collins Burke all my real property consisting of
the S/2, N/2, S/2, SW/4, NW/4, SE/4 and
the S/2, S/2, SW/4, NW/4, SE/4 and
the N/2, NW/4, SW/4, SE/4 and
the N/2, N/2, S/2, NW/4, SW/4, SE/4 of Section 32 and
the SE/4, NE/4, NW/4 and
the NE/4, SE/4, NW/4 of section 19, all of T. 2 N, R. 5 E. on
the Salt River Indian Reservation containing 30 acres.
To the said Alice Collins Burke I also bequeath 1 mare and the increase thereof.

To Benjamine Collins I bequeath 1 mare and the increase thereof.

To John Collins I bequeath all my personal property that may remain after the above bequests have been fulfilled.

This is my last will and testament and must hold in law.

Witness my hand and seal this 13th day of October, 1915.

her
Margaret Enos [thumb print]
mark

The above will and testament of Margaret Enos was made and signed in our presence this 13th day of October, 1915.

CH Ellis
Joseph L Wellington

I hereby certify that there appeared before me personally Margaret Enos, the Indian who executed the above instrument and that she swears that it is her last will and testament.

Charles E. (Illegible)

Department of The Interior,
Office of Indian Affairs, Washington, NOV 8 1919

It is hereby recommended that the within will of Margaret Enos #1, deceased Pima allottee No. 230, be approved pursuant to the provisions of the Act of June 25, 1910 (36 Stats. L., 855-6) as amended by Act of February 14, 1913 (37 Stats. L., 678).

Respectfully,
EB Meritt
Assistant Commissioner

Department of The Interior NOV 11 1919
Office of The Secretary

The within will of Margaret Enos #1, deceased Pima allottee No. 230, is hereby approved, pursuant to the provisions of the Act of June 25, 1910 (36 Stats. L., 855-6) as amended by Act of February 14, 1913 (37 Stats. L., 678).

SG Hopkins
Assistant Secretary

▲▼▲▼▲▼▲▼▲▼▲▼▲▼

WILLIS ROWLAND

Original
WILL

OFFICE OF INDIAN AFFAIRS
RECEIVED
MAY 21 1917
49939

Indian Wills, 1911 – 1921 Book Six
Records of The Bureau of Indian Affairs

I, **Willis Rowland** of Pine Ridge Agency, South Dakota, Allottee number **7333** do hereby make and declare this to be my last will and testament, in accordance with Section 2 of the Act of June 25, 1910, (36 stat. 855-858) and Act of February 14, 1913, (Public No. 381), hereby revoking all former wills made by me:

1. I hereby direct that as soon as possible after my decease, that all my debts, funeral and testamentary expenses be paid out of my personal estate.

2. I give and devise my allotment on the Pine Ridge Reservation, South Dakota, described as follows:

Lots 2, 3, 4, the S/2 of SW/4 and SW/4 of SE/4 of Sec. 24 and SE/4 of SE/4 of Section 23 all in Twp. 43 north of Range 43 west of the Sixth Principal Meridian, South Dakota, containing 308.31 acres,

in the following manner:

To my half-sister, Pearl Rowland: Lots 2 and 3, the SE/4 of SW/4 and the SW/4 of SE/4 of Section 24 in Twp. 43 N. of Range 43.

To my step-mother, Nellie Rowland: Lot 4 and the SW/4 of SW/4 of Section 24 and the SE/4 of SE/4 of Section 23 in Twp. 43 N. of Range 43 west of the Sixth Principal Meridian.

3. I give and bequeath all of my personal property of whatsoever nature and wheresoever situated unto

my half-sister, Pearl and my step-mother, Nellie Rowland, in equal shares.

4. All the rest of my property, real ~~or personal~~, now possessed or hereafter acquired, of whatsoever nature and wheresoever situated, I hereby give, devise and bequeath unto

my half-sister, Pearl Rowland.

In witness whereof I have hereunto set my hand this **12th** day of **May** 1915 .

Willis Rowland

The above statement was, this **12th** day of **May** 1915 signed and published by **Willis Rowland** as **his** last will and testament, in the joint presence of the undersigned, the said **Willis Rowland** then being of sound and vigorous mind and free from any constraint or compulsion; whereupon we, being without any interest in the matter other than friendship, and being well acquainted with **him** but not members of **his** family, immediately subscribed our names hereto in the presence of each other and of the said testator, for the purpose of attesting the said will, as **he** requested us to do.

	Post Office Address
George A Trotter	**Kyle, South Dakota.**
Jacob White Eyes	**Kyle, South Dakota.**

Pine Ridge, South Dakota.
May 16 1917

I hereby certify that I have fully inquired into the mental competency of the Indian signing the above will; the circumstances attending the execution of the will; the influence that may have induced its execution, and the names of those entitled to share in the estate under the law of descent in South Dakota: reasons for the disposition of the property proposed by the will differing from disposition had the property descended by operation of law.

I respectfully forward this will with the recommendation that it be …..approved.

WM Landman
Acting Supt. ~~& Spl. Disb. Agent.~~

Department of The Interior,
Office of Indian Affairs, Washington, APR -3 1919

It is recommended that the within will of Willis Rowland, deceased Pine Ridge Sioux allottee No. 7333, dated May 12, 1915, be approved in accordance with the Act of June 25, 1910 (36 Stats. L., 855-6) as amended by Act of February 14, 1913 (37 Stats. L., 678).

Respectfully,
EB Meritt
Assistant Commissioner

Department of The Interior
Office of The Secretary   NOV 19 1919

The within will of Willis Rowland, deceased Pine Ridge Sioux allottee No. 7333, dated May 12, 1915, is approved in accordance with the Act of June 25, 1910 (36 Stats. L., 855-6) as amended by Act of February 14, 1913 (37 Stats. L., 678).

SG Hopkins
Assistant Secretary

▲▼▲▼▲▼▲▼▲▼▲▼▲▼

ALICE MOUSSEAU nee IRON CLOUD

WILL

REC'D
MAR 15 1918
Pine Ridge Agency
S. Dak.

I, **Alice Mousseau (nee Iron Cloud)** of Pine Ridge Agency, South Dakota, Allottee number **545** do hereby make and declare this to be my last will and testament, in accordance with Section 2 of the Act of June 25, 1910, (36 stat. 855-858) and Act of February 14, 1913, (Public No. 381), hereby revoking all former wills made by me:

1. I hereby direct that as soon as possible after my decease, that all my debts, funeral and testamentary expenses be paid out of my personal estate.

2. I give and devise my allotment on the Pine Ridge Reservation, South Dakota, described as follows: **S/2 of Section 3, Twnp-38, N. Range 42 W. of the 6th P.M. in South Dakota, Containing 320 acres.**

in the following manner:

I desire to will one hundred and sixty (160) acres to my children-Luois[sic], James, David, Robert and Paul Mousseau, to be divided equally.

And one hundred and sixty (160 acres to my husband Louis X Mousseau.

3. I give and bequeath all of my personal property of whatsoever nature and wheresoever situated unto

Ten (10) head of cattle (heifers and cows) belonging to my children, with my personally brand, I desire to have my husband have supervision and retained to benefit my children. (My husband

has nine (9) head of cattle. Twelve (12) head horses belonging to my children, ten (10) to my husband, and I desire to will one *mare* to my mother (Runs For Hills).

4.   All the rest of my property, real or personal, now possessed or hereafter acquired, of whatsoever nature and wheresoever situated, I hereby give, devise and bequeath unto   **My children and My husband, I further desire to have my husband (Louis X. Mousseau) keep our children and raise them properly, and to retain all house hold goods for their benefit.**

In witness whereof I have hereunto set my hand this **12th** day of **March** 1918.   *her*

Alice Mousseau [thumb print]

mark

The above statement was, this **12th** day of **March** 1918 signed and published by **Alice Mousseau (nee Iron Cloud)** as **her** last will and testament, in the joint presence of the undersigned, the said **Alice Mousseau** then being of sound and vigorous mind and free from any constraint or compulsion; whereupon we, being without any interest in the matter other than friendship, and being well acquainted with **her** but not members of **her** family, immediately subscribed our names hereto in the presence of each other and of the said testator, for the purpose of attesting the said will, as **she** requested us to do.   And that I, **Chas. D. Parkhurst,** at the testa.....'s request, have written **her** name in ink, and that **I** affixed **her** thumb-marks.

	Post Office Address
Chas. D. Parkhurst	**Porcupine, S.D.**
Oliver J. Eagle	**Porcupine, S.D.**

Pine Ridge, South Dakota.
October 9, 1918.
    I hereby certify that I have fully inquired into the mental competency of the Indian signing the above will; the circumstances attending the execution of the will; the influence that may have induced its execution, and the names of those entitled to share in the estate under the law of descent in South Dakota: reasons for the disposition of the property proposed by the will differing from disposition had the property descended by operation of law.

I respectfully forward this will with the recommendation that it be
.....approved.

Henry M. Tidwell
Supt. & Spl. Disb. Agent.

Department of The Interior,
Office of Indian Affairs, Washington,
DEC 23 1919

The within will of Alice Mousseau otherwise known as Alice Iron Cloud
is hereby recommended for approval in accordance with the Act of June
25, 1910 (36 Stats. L., 855-6) as amended by Act of February 14, 1913
(37 Stats. L., 678).

EB Meritt
Assistant Commissioner

Department of The Interior
Office of The Secretary DEC 24 1919

The within will is hereby approved in accordance with the provisions of
the Act of June 25, 1910 (36 Stats. L., 855-6) as amended by Act of
February 14, 1913 (37 Stats. L., 678).

SG Hopkins
Assistant Secretary

▲▼▲▼▲▼▲▼▲▼▲▼▲▼

MRS. BAT RICHARD or ROSA RICHARD

Mrs. Bat Richard's Will.

Nov 1ˢᵗ 1918

Henry Richard
1 Sorrell Mare with colt
1 Grey   "   "   "
1 Mare with colt given her by Jas. H. Wing

Sousie Richard
1 Grey mare with colt
1 Black   "   "   "

Lillian Richard
1 White mare with 2 colts

1 Bay mare with 1 colt
1 Bay mare & set big harness

Joseph Richard will take care of all of the land and sell all of the crops.

The house is on my land half section
I give this to my oldest daughter so that when she gets married she can improve the land and take care of her little brother and sister
And my oldest daughter shall make her home with Mrs. Mary White Rabbit, until such time as she gets married. And that Mrs. Mary White Rabbit shall do all of the childs[sic] buisness[sic] until she becomes of age. And Sousie shall also make her home with her sister at Mrs. Mary White Rabits[sic] place. And Henry Richard shall make his home with Peter Richard his Grandfather.

Mrs Bat Richard

Witness   Walter Young
*   Joseph La Point*

Department of The Interior,
Office of Indian Affairs, Washington,
                    JAN -6 1920
The within will of Mrs. Bat Richard or Rosa Richard, is hereby recommended for approval in accordance with the Act of June 25, 1910 (36 Stats. L., 855-6) as amended by Act of February 14, 1913 (37 Stats. L., 678).

                            Respectfully,
                            EB Meritt
                            Assistant Commissioner

Department of The Interior
Office of The Secretary

The within will is hereby approved in accordance with the Act of June 25, 1910 (36 Stats. L., 855-6) as amended by Act of February 14, 1913 (37 Stats. L., 678).

                            SG Hopkins
                            Assistant Secretary

▲▼▲▼▲▼▲▼▲▼▲▼▲▼▲▼

<u>**MINNIE AH-KAUN**</u>

LAST WILL AND TESTAMENT

Anadarko, Okla.
April 6, 1917.

I, Minnie Ah-kaun, of Anadarko, Oklahoma, Kiowa Indian allottee No. 314, of sound and disposing mind, but sensible of the uncertainty of live[sic] and desiring to make disposition of my property and affairs while in health, do hereby make, publish and declare the following to be my last will and testament, hereby revoking and cancelling all other and former wills by me at any time made.

1.   I direct the payment of all my just debts and funeral expenses.

2nd.   I give and devise to my husband William V. Burns the sum of $1.00 and specifically direct that this is the only devise made to him and that he is not to share in any other property of which I may desire possessed.

3rd.   I give and devise in equal shares all of my property of which I may die possessed, including my trust allotment of land and the allotments to which I am a part heir, as well as all other property, real and personal of which I may die possessed, to the following persons:

a.   To my mother Ah-kann, Kiowa Indian allottee No. 313.

b.   To my Aunt, Dome-gat-ty, Kiowa Indian allottee No. 308.

c.   To my beloved half sister Frankie Tsait-kope-ta, Kiowa Indian Allottee No. 2841.

d.   To my beloved half brother, William Paul Zumwalt, an unallotted Kiowa Indian, son of Claud Zumwalt, a white man and Au-kaun, Kiowa allottee No. 313, my mother.

The above includes the following trust property in which each of the last four named beneficiaries are to share equally so that each will take 1/4 interest in and to my estate:

All of my interest in and to the South-west quarter of section 21[sic], Township 7N, of Range 10 West of the I.M., being known upon the rolls of the Interior Department as Kiowa Indian allotment No. 307. This land was allotted to Tsait-kope-ta, now dead, of whose estate in L-H-153534-13 E.G.T., I was declared to be an heir to the extent of one-third thereof.

All of my interest in and to the North-East Quarter of Section 31, Township 7N, of Range 10W, of the IM known upon the rolls of the Interior Department as Kiowa allotment No. 315. This land was allotted to Thomas Ah-kaun, now dead, and of whose estate, in L-H-66260-1915, F.E. I was declared to be an heir to the estent[sic] of one-third thereof.

All of my interest in and to the fractional North West Quarter of Section 31, Township 7 North, of Range 10 West of the I.M. known upon the rolls of the Interior Department as Kiowa Indian allotment No. 311. This land was allotted to William Paul Tsait-kope-ta, now dead, and of whose estate, in L-H-66261-15, F.E., I was declared to be an heir to the estent[sic] of one-sixth thereof.

All of my interest in and to the North-East Quarter of Section 19, Township 5 North, of Range 11 W., of the I.M., known upon the rolls of the Interior Department as Kiowa Indian allotment No. 309. This land was allotted to Ah-to-kei-ah, now dead, of whose estate in L-H-153535-13 E.G.T. I was declared to be an heir, to the extent of one-third thereof.

All of my interest in and to the South-East quarter of Section 19, Township 5 North, of Range 11 W., of the I.M., Known upon the rolls of the Interior Department as Kiowa allotment No. 312. This land was allotted to James Tsait-kope-ta, now dead, of whose estate, in L-H-153536-13 E.G.T., I was declared to be an heir to the estent[sic] of one-third thereof.

This will is made subject to the approval of the Secretary of the Interior.

In witness whereof, I, Minnie Au-kaun, have to this my last will and testament, consisting of three (3) sheets of paper, subscribed my name this 6th day of April, 1917, at Anadarko, Oklahoma.

Minnie Ah-Kaun

Subscribed by Minnie Au-kaun in the presence of each of us the undersigned and at the same time declared by her to us to be her last will and testament and we thereupon at the request of Minnie Au-kaun, in her presence and in the presence of each other, sign our names hereto as witnesses, this 6th day of April, 1917, at Anadarko, Oklahoma.

HG Wilson
Roseburg, Oregon
Post Office
PA Romick
Anadarko, Okla
Post Office

AFFIDAVIT TO ACCOMPANY WILL.

State of Oklahoma,
County of Caddo.

I, Minnie Au-kaun, first having been duly sworn state; that I have this day made a last will and testament in which I devise $1.00 only to my husband William V. Burns and it is my intention that he shall not share in any of the property of which I may die possessed; that this will was made and I now direct that said $1.00 shall be all to which said husband shall be entitled after my death; that my reason for the devise is that my said husband abandoned me, that he never supported me while married and living with him and that he did not nurse or care for me during my illness.

For the above reasons I request that the Department approve my will. It was made after mature deliberation.

Minnie Ah-Kaun

Subscribed and sworn to before me this 6th day of April, 1917,

H.E. Bretschneider
Notary Public

My commission expires March 26, 1921.

APPROVAL OF WILL

Department of The Interior,
Office of Indian Affairs, Washington,

JAN 19 1920

The within will of Minnie Ah-kaun, deceased Kiowa allottee No. 314, is hereby recommended for approval in accordance with the provisions of the Act of June 25, 1910 (36 Stats. L., 855-6) as amended by Act of February 14, 1913 (37 Stats. L., 678).

EB Meritt
Assistant Commissioner

Department of The Interior
Office of The Secretary JAN 26 1920

Pursuant to the provisions of Act of June 25, 1910 (36 Stats. L., 855-6) as amended by Act of February 14, 1913 (37 Stats. L., 678) and the Regulations of the Department, I hereby approve the within will of Minnie Ah-kaun, deceased Kiowa allottee No. 314.

SG Hopkins
Assistant Secretary

GEORGE SICKMAN

**** W I L L ****

OFFICE OF INDIAN AFFAIRS
RECEIVED
FEB 15 1915
18540

IN THE NAME OF GOD, AMEN:

I, GEORGE SICKMAN, an Indian of the Quiniault Reserve Chehalis County, in the State of Washington, of the age of about sixty (60) years and married, being of sound and disposing mind and memory and not acting under duress, menace, fraud or undue influence of any person or persons whatsoever, do make, publish and declare this my LAST WILL AND TESTAMENT in manner following, hereby revoking any and all wills made heretofore by me.

I direct that all my just debts and obligations be paid first and to that end I nominate and appoint ALICE JACKSON, an Indian woman, as Executrix of this my LAST WILL AND TESTAMENT and I direct that in case of my death she be and is hereby empowered to take, hold and be seized and possessed of, and vested with the title of my estate for the purpose of carrying into effect this will, and without the further intervention of any Court or of the issuance of any Letters Testamentary or of Administration except to admit this will to Probate and to cause a true inventory of the property of the estate to be filed and notice be published to creditors, all subject to the will of the Indian Department of the United States Government.

I hereby expressly provide that no Bond be given for security and so far as in any case may be the said Executrix, Alice Jackson, be and she is hereby relieved from the supervision of all Courts.

I hereby direct in order that all my just debts be paid and in the settlement of my said estate the said Executrix be and she is empowered to make any and all contracts, sales and other instruments necessary to carry out the provisions of my Will.

After the payment of all my just debts and obligations, I give and devise and bequeath all of my property of every kind, name and description, of all kinds both real and personal and especially my Fishing Rights given to me by the United States Government on the Quiniault River, to my wife MARY SICKMAN. I have no children and all my property shall go to my wife.

I further direct that the said ALICE JACKSON care for and provide for my said wife, and that she be paid a reasonable compensation for so doing, and that she continue to handle said estate until such time as she thinks best to close the same with the approval of the proper authority of the United States Government.

IN WITNESS WHEREOF, I have hereunto set my hand and seal this Second day of February, A.D. 1915. *His right*

George [thumb print] *Sickman*
thumb mark

The foregoing instrument consisting of one page and a quarter is the LAST WILL AND TESTAMENT of GEORGE SICKMAN, and was on the day and year above written, signed, sealed, published and declared to be his Last Will and Testament by the said George Sickman in the presence of us, who, at his request and in his presence, and in the presence of each other, have subscribed our names as witnesses thereto, and we do hereby solemnly certify that the said George Sickman was not acting under duress or restraint and was of sound and disposing mind and memory.

> *L.H. Brewer*
> Occupation *Lawyer*
> Residing at Hoquiam, Chehalis Co. Wash.
> *L.N. Taff*
> Occupation *Bookeeper*[sic]
> Residing at Hoquiam, Chehalis Co. Wash.
> *H.W. Bale*
> Occupation *Lumberman*
> Residing at Hoquiam, Chehalis Co. Wash.

Department of The Interior,
Office of Indian Affairs, Washington,
APR -1 1915

The within will of George Sickman, Quinaielt allottee No. 71 is hereby recommended for approval pursuant to the provisions of the Act of February 14, 1913 (37 Stats. L., 678).

> Respectfully,
> *EB Meritt*
> Assistant Commissioner

Department of The Interior
Office of The Secretary APR -2 1915

The within will of George Sickman, Quinaielt allottee No. 71, is hereby approved pursuant to the provisions of the Act of February 14, 1913 (37 Stats. L., 678).

> *Bo Sweeney*
> Assistant Secretary

▲▼▲▼▲▼▲▼▲▼▲▼▲▼

CHRISTOPHER COLUMBUS GOGGLES

I Christopher Columbus Goggles having the full use of reason, of my own free will hereby bequeath and bequest to my lawful wife Lucy W. Goggles forty acres of my allotment, these forty acres to be chosen by herself.

I also bequeath and bequest to my wife Lucy W. Goggles, the eight acres of land which I inherited from my father.

47

Moreover, I bequeath and bequest to my brother Benjamin Goggles forty acres of my allotment.   His

Christopher C Goggles [thumb print]
mark

St. Stephen's February 10, 1917.

We the undersigned witnesses hereby testify on honor that the above thumb mark is the mark of Christopher C. Goggles made by him of his own free will.

x *Alonzo Moss*
x *Benjamin Warren*
W.C. Hopkins

PROBATE
46658-1918
79488-1919
  L L

Department of The Interior,
Office of Indian Affairs, Washington, JAN 26 1920

It is recommended that the within will be approved in pursuance of the provisions of the Act of June 25, 1910 (36 Stats. L., 855-6) as amended by Act of February 14, 1913 (37 Stats. L., 678).

Respectfully,
EB Meritt
Assistant Commissioner

Department of The Interior FEB -9 1920
Office of The Secretary

The within will is hereby approved in pursuance of the provisions of the Act of June 25, 1910 (36 Stats. L., 855-6) as amended by Act of February 14, 1913 (37 Stats. L., 678).

Franklin K Payne
Assistant Secretary

OFFICE OF INDIAN AFFAIRS
RECEIVED
NOV -8 1919
95952

LOUIS LA SARGE

LAST WILL AND TESTAMENT OF LOUIS LA SARGE.

I, the undersigned, Louis La Sarge of Arkansas City, Cowley County, Kansas, and Menteca, San Joaquin County, California, do hereby make, publish and declare this my last Will and Testament in the manner and form following:

FIRST: I request and direct that all my just debts and funeral expenses be paid as soon after my decease as can conveniently be done.

SECOND: I hereby give, devise and bequeath to my beloved wife Letitia La Sarge of Menteca, San Joaquin County California, the residence and the real estate on which it is located in the town of Menteca, San Joaquin County, California, being the only residence or real estate owned by me in the State of California and the household goods, furnishings and furniture therein located, to have and to hold the same to her absolutely and forever.

THIRD: I hereby give, devise and bequeath to my beloved wife Letitia La Sarge of Menteca, San Joaquin County, California, the full undivided One Third of all the rest, residue and remainder of my property both real and personal wheresoever situated of which I may die possessed and to which I may be entitled being principally about Six Hundred and Fifty-four acres of land in Osage County, Oklahoma and my rights, property and assets as a member of the Osage Indian, including Oil and Gas bonus royalties and any and all moneys and funds due and to become due me from the United States Government of as a member of said Osage Indians and any and all personal and real property of which I may die seized and in possession to have and to hold the same to her absolutely and forever.

FOURTH: I hereby give, devise and bequeath the full two-thirds of all the said rest, residue and remainder of the property of which I may die seized and possessed both real and personal wheresoever situated being principally as above mentioned in Paragraph Three hereof to William Bunnell of Arkansas City, Cowley County, Kansas, in trust for the uses and pruposes[sic] herein mentioned to have and to hold, possess, manage and control and operate the same with full power in my said Trustee or successors of him to obtain, receive and hold, possess, and manage all the incomes, rents, interest and profits derived from the management, operation and control thereof with full power in my said trustee or the successors of him to rent, lease, manage, handle, invest and loan and re-invest and re-loan said property without the authority or order of any Court and with full power to invest or re-invest said moneys coming into his hands as said Trustee in the best manner as he may deem to the best interest of the Estate and trust hereby created and with full power to pay all taxes, interest, insurance and keep up repairs on all property that may come into his hands as such, hereby releaving[sic] the Trustee from any liability in any errors in judgment in the management and control of any investments thereof so long as he acts in good faith and I further direct that said trustee as soon after my decease as can conveniently be done apply to the proper Court to have a bond fixed as such Trustee of said Estate and Trust and that for his services thereabouts or his successors in trust be allowed such sum of money from time to time as to the Court fixing said bond shall seem meet and proper and that during the minority of my Son Robert Louis La Sarge of Menteca, California said Trustee out of said trustee property and funds and particularly the profit and income therefore pay out and use for said son such sum or moneys from time to time as are necessary and proper for said childs[sic] maintenance and education and comforts suitable to one in his station in life, considering the amount of the estate or other facts and circumstances ordinarily to be given consideration in determining such maintenance, education and comforts and luxries[sic] and that upon my said son reaching his majority, the trustee to deliver over to my said son all of said estate and trust property real and personal and all incomes, profits and incomes thereof less the necessary expenses incured[sic] and necessary for such compensation as may be the court be allowed, and said estate and trust property real and personal thereupon be delivered and vested in my said son Robert Louis La Sarge to have and to hold the same to him absolutely and forever.

FIFTH: I hereby authorize and direct that in the event of the incapacity or death of my said Trustee William Bunnell that the District Court of Osage County, Oklahoma or the Judge thereof appoint a suitable successor in trust, he giving such bond as such Court or Judge deems sufficient and proper.

SIXTH: I hereby nominate and appoint *William Bunnell Arkansas City, Ks.* Executor of this my Lat Will and Testament and direct that he act without bond and request that he close my estate in the proper Court or courts and make the division and distribution as herein provided as soon after my death as can conveniently be done.

SEVENTH: I hereby revoke any former and other Wills and Testamentary dispositions by me heretofore made.

IN WITNESS Whereof, I have hereunto subscribed my name and affixed my seal this 25th day of July, 1918, at Arkansas City, Kansas, in the presence of *C L Swarts* of Arkansas City, Kansas, and *Ed J (Illegible)* of Arkansas City, Kansas whom I have requested to be witnesses hereto.

Louis La Sarge

(SEAL)

The foregoing instrument was subscribed, sealed, published and declared by Louis La Sarge as and for his last Will and Testament in our presence and in the presence of each of us and we at the same time at his request and in his presence and in the presence of each other hereunto subscribed our names and addresses as attesting witnesses hereto this 25th day of July, 1918.

CL Swarts
Arkansas City Kansas
Ed J (Illegible)
Arkansas City, Kansas

I hereby nominate and appoint my Mother Bertha Bunnell Guardian of the person of my son Robert Louis La Sarge in the event of the death of my wife Letitia La Sarge at any time prior to my said son reaching full age & request that in such event my said mother be so appointed and given the care and custody of my said son.

Witness my hand this 25 day of July, 1918.

Louis LaSarge

Witnesses
CLSwarts
Ed J *(Illegible)*

Probate
95952-19
L L

Approval of Will
Osage Agency, Okla.

Department of The Interior,
Office of Indian Affairs, Washington,
                    JAN 23 1920

The within will of Louis LaSarge, Osage allottee No. 1421, is hereby recommended for approval in accordance with the provisions of the Act of April 18, 1912, (37 Stat. L. 86-88) as to all property under the jurisdiction of the United States.

Respectfully,
EB Meritt
Assistant Commissioner

Department of The Interior
Office of The Secretary FEB 11 1920

The within will of Louis LaSarge, Osage allottee No. 1421, is hereby approved in accordance with the provisions of the Act of April 18, 1912, (37 Stat. L. 86-88) as to property over which the United States has jurisdiction.

Franklin K Payne
~~Assistant~~ Secretary

▲▼▲▼▲▼▲▼▲▼▲▼▲▼

PAU-KUNE

I, Pau-Kune, of lawful age, of Lement, Caddo County Oklahoma, do hereby make, publish and declare this my last Will and Testament in manner and form following:

First: I direct that all my just debts and funeral expenses be paid as soon after my decease as conveniently can be done.

Second: I give, devise and bequeath to my son, Jose Pau-Kune, an undivided two-thirds (2/3) interest in and to the following described real estate situate[sic] in Caddo County Oklahoma, to wit: The South east quarter of the south west quarter (SE1/4 of SW1/4) and the Southwest quarter of the South East quarter (SW1/4 of SE1/4) of Section Three (3) and the North half of the Northeast quarter (N1/2 of NE1/4) of Section Ten (10) in Township Five (5) North of Range Nine (9) West of the Indian Meridian in Oklahoma containing one hundred and sixty acres to have and to hold the same to him absolutely and forever.

Third: I give, devise and bequeath to my wife Juann Pau-Kune an undivided one-third (1/3) interest in and to the following described real estate situate in Caddo County, Oklahoma, to-wit: The South east quarter of the South west quarter (SE1/4 of SW1/4) of Section Three (3) and the North half of the north east quarter (N1/2 of NE1/4) of Section Ten (10) in Township Five (5) north of Range Nine (9) west of the Indian Meridian in Oklahoma, containing one hundred and sixty acres, to have and to hold the same to her absolutely and forever.

Fourth: I give and bequeath to Arthur Cruz the sum of Five (5) dollars.

Fifth: All the rest, residue and remainder of of[sic] my estate, real, personal and mixed wheresoever situate, of which I may die seized or possessed, or to which I may be entitled at the time of my decease, I give, devise and bequeath to my wife Juann Pau-Kune, and to my son Jose Pau-Kune, share and share alike to have and to hold the same to them absolutely and forever.

*Sixth: It is my wish that my family live upon and occupy the land herein above described **as their home** until my son Jose shall become of age.*

Seventh: I hereby revoke all former wills heretofore made by me.

In Witness Whereof, I have hereunto subscribed my name, at my farm Neon Cement in Caddo County, Oklahoma, this Twelvth[sic] day of March, A.D. 1919 in the presence of Sotaro Rooch, Ben Rooch, and CH Canswell, whom I have requested to become attesting witnesses hereto.

Witness to mark:	*his*
At the request of the said	*Pau- X Kune* [thumb print]
Pau-Kune, I wrote his name	*mark*
and witnessed his mark.	
CH Carswell	

The foregoing instrument was subscribed, published and declared by Pau-Kune, as and for his last Will and Testament, in our presence and in the presence of each and all of us, and we, at the same time, at his request, in his presence, and in the presence of each other, hereunto subscribe our names and residences as attesting witnesses this Twelvth[sic] day of March A.D. 1919.

	his
Sotero Roach	*Ben X Roach* [thumb print]
Anadarko, Okla	*mark Anadarko, Okla.*

C.H. Carswell
Residence Anadarko, Okla

et the request of Ben Roach
y Rot hes name en wytenessed
his mark [all above sic]

John Rivaz
Anadarko Okla

Probate
94138-19
7440-20
L L

Department of The Interior,
Office of Indian Affairs, Washington,
JAN -2 1920

The within will of Pau-kune, deceased Apache, allottee No. 951, is hereby recommended for approval in accordance with the provisions of the Act of June 25, 1910 (36 Stats. L., 855-6) as amended by Act of February 14, 1913 (37 Stats. L., 678).

Very Respectfully,
EB Meritt
Assistant Commissioner

Department of The Interior
Office of The Secretary FEB 14 1920

Pursuant to the provisions of Act of June 25, 1910 (36 Stats. L., 855-6) and the regulations of the Department, I hereby approve the within will of Pau-kune, deceased Apache allottee No. 951.

Franklin K Payne
Secretary

▲▼▲▼▲▼▲▼▲▼▲▼▲▼▲▼

BENJAMIN ISAAC

DEPARTMENT OF THE INTERIOR

UNITED STATES INDIAN SERVICE
Wellpinit, Wash., Oct. 8, 1917.

KNOW ALL MEN BY THESE PRESENTS:

That I, Benj. Isac[sic] being of sound mind and disposing memory, feeble in body, and desiring to arrange my affairs finally do hereby make this my last will and testament as follows:-

To John Isador, my nephew, to Osiah Winn, my nephew, and to Lily Martin, my niece, all my real estate consisting of my allotment on the Spokane Reservation, to share and share equally. All my personal property consisting of three head of horses and one colt, one wagon and harness, one mower, to be given to my nephew Osiah Winn, upon whom it is enjoined to pay all my debts, give my fitting burial in case of death, and place a suitable stone at my grave. It is my will that my wife shall have no interest in my estate for the reason that she deserted me a year ago.

Signed in duplicate before:

Witnesses:

(Signature Illegible)
  Wellpinit, Wash

(Signature Illegible)
  Wellpinit, Wash   His
                                        Benj. Isaac [thumb print]
                                                             Mark

Department of The Interior,
Office of Indian Affairs, Washington,
                    FEB -5 1920
The within will of Benjamin Isaac, Spokane allottee No. 64, is hereby recommended for approval in accordance with the provisions of the Act of June 25, 1910 (36 Stats. L., 855-6).
                              Respectfully,
                              EB Meritt
                              Assistant Commissioner
Department of The Interior
Office of The Secretary FEB 11 1920

The within will of Benjamin Isaac, Spokane allottee No. 64, is hereby approved pursuant to the provisions of the Act of June 25, 1910 (36 Stats. L., 855-6).

Franklin K Payne
Secretary

▲▼▲▼▲▼▲▼▲▼▲▼

JOSEPH LUMPRY

OFFICE OF INDIAN AFFAIRS
RECEIVED
JUN 26 1916
69311

IN THE NAME OF GOD, AMEN:

BE IT REMEMBERED THAT I, Joseph Lumpry, Flathead Allottee No. 1240, now a resident of the Flathead Indian Reservation in the County of Missoula, and State of Montana, of the age of 66 years, being of sound and disposing mind and memory, and not acting under duress, fraud, or under the influence of any person whomsoever, do make, publish and declare this, my last will and testament, in the following manner, that is to say:

I leave will and devise to Adel Gebeau, my daughter, and only heir, my interest in the land I have inherited from my deceased wife, Louise Lumpry, being a one-third interest in the W1/2 of the NW1/4 of Sec. 35, T. 17 N., R. 20 W., E.M., also all other inherited interests I may possess at the time of my death; also all of my personal property and what funds I have held in trust for me.

I hereby nominate and appoint Adel Gebeau of Arlee, Montana, the executor of this, my last will and testament, and I hereby revoke all former wills by me made.

In witness whereof, I have hereunto set my hand and seal this *17* day of June, in the year of our Lord, One Thousand Nine Hundred and Sixteen.   his
Joseph Lumpry [thumb print]
mark

The foregoing instrument, consisting of this one page, was, at the date thereof, by said Joseph Lumpry, signed, sealed, and published as, and declared to be his last will and testament, in the presence of us, who, at his request, and in his presence and in the presence of each other, have hereunto subscribed our names as witnesses thereto.
Corrie Hiatt, Farmer
Witnesses are also witnesses to mark:
Charles D. Faunce, Dep. Sup. For (Illegible) Both of Arlee, Mont.

Department of The Interior,
Office of Indian Affairs, Washington,
SEP 27 1916

The within will of is hereby recommended for approval in accordance with the provisions of the Act of June 25, 1910 (36 Stats. L., 855-6) as amended by Act of February 14, 1913 (37 Stats. L., 678).

EB Meritt
Assistant Commissioner

Department of The Interior
Office of The Secretary OCT -4 1916

The within will of is hereby approved in accordance with the provisions of the Act of June 25, 1910 (36 Stats. L., 855-6) as amended by Act of February 14, 1913 (37 Stats. L., 678).

Bo Sweeney
Assistant Secretary

OFFICE OF INDIAN AFFAIRS
RECEIVED
JAN 12 1920
3040

JOHN ALLEN

I, John Allen, being of full age and of sound and desposing[sic] mind and memory do declare this to be my last will and testament.

    1st.   I direct that all my just debts be paid.

    2nd.   I will and bequeth all my property of which I may die seized as follows to with[sic]

    Funds on deposit in the Toledo Savings Bank, same being held under supervision of the Superintendent of the Sac & Fox Sanatorium, Toledo, Iowa, as Individual Indian Money, and my undivided one-half interest in five room frame house located on the Sac & Fox, Iowa Reservation, to my sister, Na-to-wa-se-qua.

    I hereby nominate the Superintendent of the Sac & Fox Reservation to be executor without bond of this my last will and testament this 18th day of July, 1917.

his
John Allen [thumb print]
thumb

Witness.

> *Robt Lyons*
> *Toledo, Ia*
> *R Graves*
> *Toledo, Iowa*

We hereby certify that on this 18th day of July, 1917, at the Sac & Fox Sanatorium, in Tama County, Iowa, John Allen to us personally known did in our presence make the foregoing instrument and declare the same to be his last will and testament and we at his request and in his presence and in the presence of each other do subscribe our names as witness thereto.

> *Robt. Lyons*
> *Toledo, Ia*
> *R. Graves*
> *Toledo, Iowa*

Probate
13317-19
3340-1920
W H G

Department of The Interior,
Office of Indian Affairs, Washington, AUG 31 1916

It is recommended that the within will of John Allen, deceased, be approved under the Act of June 25, 1910 (36 Stats. L., 855-6) as amended by Act of February 14, 1913 (37 Stats. L., 678), and the Regulations of the Department.

> Respectfully,
> *EB Meritt*
> AUG 31 1916   Assistant Commissioner

Department of The Interior
Office of The Secretary

The within will of John Allen, deceased, is hereby approved under the Act of June 25, 1910 (36 Stats. L., 855-6) as amended by Act of February 14, 1913 (37 Stats. L., 678).

> *Alexander T Vogelsburg*
> First Assistant Secretary

▲▼▲▼▲▼▲▼▲▼▲▼▲▼▲▼

NO TEETH or NO FEATHER

I, No Teeth or No Feather, a member of the Sioux Tribe of the Cheyenne River Agency, and being of sound mind, make this my last Will and Testament. I give, devise and bequeth my estate and property, real and personal, as follows:

> TO=Henry Grouse Running, the following;
>> All I.D. Stuff, which includes the following:
>> 1 wagon, 1 set double harness, 1 plow, 1 harrow,
>> 2 mares, 2 cows and 1 calf.

> TO=Henry Grouse Running, Ray Eagle Chasing, Peter Holy
>> Bull, and Flora Paterson, the following:
>> S.E. Quarter of Section 21, Range 18, Township 12.

> TO=Thomas Eagle Chasing, the following;
>> N.E. Quarter of Section 21, Range 18, Township 12.

Signed and acknowledged this 3rd of August, A.D. 1915.

her

Signed,   *No Teeth or No Feather* [thumb print]

mark

Finton Rueley)
)
) Witnesses.
)
James Brown)

Cheyenne River Agency, S.D.

RECEIVED

AUG 9 1915

Sworn to me this 3rd day of August, A.D. 1915.

G.M. Griffiths Notary Public.

Dated at Cherry Creek, S.D.

on **3**   day **Aug.**   1915.

MAR 17 1920

Department of The Interior,
Office of Indian Affairs, Washington,

The Office recommends that the within will of No Teeth or No Feather, Cheyenne River Sioux allottee No. 1416, executed on August 3, 1915, be approved under the Act of June 25, 1910 (36 Stats. L., 855-6) as amended by Act of February 14, 1913 (37 Stats. L., 678).

Respectfully,
EB Meritt
Assistant Commissioner

Department of The Interior
Office of The Secretary MAR 20 1920

The within will of No Teeth or No Feather, Cheyenne River Sioux allottee No. 1416, executed on August 3, 1915, is hereby approved under the Act of June 25, 1910 (36 Stats. L., 855-6) as amended by Act of February 14, 1913 (37 Stats. L., 678).

SG Hopkins
ASSISTANT Secretary

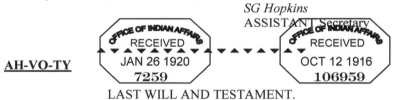

AH-VO-TY

OFFICE OF INDIAN AFFAIRS
RECEIVED
JAN 26 1920
7259

OFFICE OF INDIAN AFFAIRS
RECEIVED
OCT 12 1916
106959

LAST WILL AND TESTAMENT.

I, Ah-vo-ty, Kiowa Indian allottee No. 2414, of Mount Scott, Comanche County, Oklahoma, being now in good health, strength of body and mind, but sensible of the uncertainty of life, and desiring to make disposition of my property and affairs while in health and strength, do hereby make, publish and declare the following to be my last will and testament, hereby revoking and cancelling all other and former wills by me at any time made:

1st. I direct the payment of all my just debts and funeral expenses.

2nd. I give and devise to my niece, Julia Given Hunt, Kiowa Indian allottee No. 2813, my trust allotment of land, comprising the Fraction Northeast Quarter of Section Four (4), Township Four (4) North of Range Fourteen (14), West of the Indian Meridian in Oklahoma, Known upon the rolls of the Interior Department as Kiowa Indian allotment No. 2414.

3rd. I give and devise to Virginia Sah-maunt, Kiowa Indian allottee No. 2718, all of my interest in and to the Southeast Quarter of Section Four (4) Township Four (4) North of Range Fourteen (14), West of the Indian Meridian in Oklahoma, known upon the rolls of the Interior Department as Kiowa Indian allotment No. 1709. In this allotment I was declared to be an heir in decree of the Department, Law-Heirship 75898-1914, to the extent of one-half thereof.

4th. I give and bequeath all the rest, residue and remainder of my property, real and personal, two-thirds thereof to my said Niece, Julia Given Hunt, Kiowa Allottee No. 2813, and one-third thereof to Virginia Sah-maunt, Kiowa Allottee No. 2718.

This will is made subject to the approval of the Secretary of the Interior.

In witness whereof, I, Ah-vo-ty, have to this my last will and testament, consisting of three sheets of paper, subscribed my name this *31ˢᵗ* day of *July* 1916.

her

Ah-vo-ty [thumb print]

mark

Witness:
    Spencer Hilton
    H.E. Bretschneider

Subscribed by Ah-vo-ty in the presence of each of us, the undersigned, and at the same time declared by her to us to be her last will and testament, and we thereupon, at the request of Ah-vo-ty, in her presence and in the presence of each other, sign our names hereto as witnesses this *31ˢᵗ* day of *July*, 1916, at *Anadarko*, *Caddo* County.

Spencer Hilton
Anadarko, Okla
H.E. Bretschneider
Anadarko, Okla.

INTERPRETER'S CERTIFICATE

I, *Jasper Saunkeah* , hereby certify on honor that I acted as Interpreter during the execution of the forgoing will by Ah-vo-ty; that she fully understands all the terms and effects thereof, and that the same was drawn strictly in accordance with her desires and directions.

That I speak both the Kiowa Indian and the English languages fluently, and that I have no interest in this matter whatsoever.

Signed this *31* day of *July*, 1916.

Jasper Saunkeah
Interpreter.

Department of The Interior,
Office of Indian Affairs, Washington,
JAN 10 1917

The within will, dated July 31, 1916, of Ah-vo-ty, Kiowa allottee No. 2414, is hereby recommended for approval in pursuance of the Act of June 25, 1910 (36 Stats. L., 855-6) as amended by Act of February 14, 1913 (37 Stats. L., 678).

Respectfully,
EB Meritt
Assistant Commissioner

Department of The Interior
Office of The Secretary JAN 11 1917

The within will of Ah-vo-ty, Kiowa allottee No. 2414, is hereby recommended for approval in pursuance of the Act of June 25, 1910 (36 Stats. L., 855-6) as amended by Act of February 14, 1913 (37 Stats. L., 678).

Bo Sweeney
Assistant Secretary

Department of The Interior,
Office of Indian Affairs, Washington,
FEB 20 1920

It is recommended that Department action of January 11, 1917, approving the will of Ah-vo-ty be revoked under Act of June 25, 1910 (36 Stats. L., 855-6) as amended by Act of February 14, 1913 (37 Stats. L., 678).

Respectfully,

EB Meritt

Assistant Commissioner

Department of The Interior

Office of The Secretary   MAR 13 1920

Department action of Jan. 11, 1917, approving the will of Ah-vo-ty, is hereby revoked under the act of June 25, 1910 (36 Stats. L., 855-6) as amended by Act of February 14, 1913 (37 Stats. L., 678).

SG Hopkins

ASSISTANT Secretary

▲ ▼ ▲ ▼ ▲ ▼ ▲ ▼ ▲ ▼ ▲ ▼ ▲ ▼ ▲ ▼

SEEKING LAND or MAKOHNIHDE

LAST WILL AND TESTAMENT

OF

SEEKING LAND

OFFICE OF INDIAN AFFAIRS
RECEIVED
MAR 27 1920
26458

IN THE NAME OF GOD, AMEN.

I, Seeking land, or Makohnihda, of Crow Creek Indian Reservation, Crow Creek, Buffalo County, South Dakota, being of sound mind, memory and understanding, do hereby make and publish this my last will and testament, hereby revoking and annulling all wills by me heretofore made, and especially the will made on March 14, 1914, in manner and form following, that is to say:

First: I direct that all my just debts and funeral expenses and expenses of my last illness shall be paid as soon after my decease as shall be convenient.

Second: I give, devise and bequeath to my wife, Lena Drifting Goose, and my son, Gregory Seeking Land, both of Crow Creek Reservation, South Dakota, all of my allotment described as follows: The W1/2 of NE1/4 and the NW1/4 of section 17, and the E1/2 of NE1/4 of section 18, township 107 N., Range 71 W, 5th principal meridian, containing 320 acres, each to take the following described portion as his or her share:

Indian Wills, 1911 – 1921 Book Six
Records of The Bureau of Indian Affairs

To my wife, Lena Drifting Goose, the W1/2 of NE1/4 and E1/2 of NW1/4 of section 17, T 107 N., R 71 W., 5th P.M.,

To my son, Gregory Seeking Land, the W1/2 of NW1/4 of section 17 and the E1/2 of NE1/4 of section 18, T 107 N., R 71 W., 5th P.M.

Third: I give, devise and bequeath to my wife, Lena Drifting Goose, the SW1/4 of the NW1/4 of section 15, T 107 N., R 71 W, 5th P.M., and to My son Gregory Seeking Land the NW1/4 of the NW1/4 of section 15, T 107 N., R 71 W., 5th P.M., these tracts constituting a part of my inherited lands.

Fourth: I give, devise and bequeath to my wife, Lena Drifting Goose and my son Gregory Seeking Land, all of the allotment of Icicanape and all of the allotment of Icicahidawin, both allotments on the Sisseton Reservation and to which I am an heir, and direct that said lands be sold and the proceeds divided equally between my said wife and son.

Fifth: I give, devise and bequeath unto my wife, Lena Drifting Goose and my son Gregory Seeking Land, all my horses and cattle, farm implements, household goods, money in band, and all the rest and residue of my estate, both real and personal and mixed, to be divided between them share and share alike as nearly as may be possible.

AND LASTLY, I do not appoint an executor of this my last will and teatament[sic] for the reason that I am satisfied that the Officers of the Department of the Interior will properly dispose of my estate according to my will.

I have only one son living and no grand-children, or children of deceased children. My wife, Lena Drifting Goose and I were married at the Catholic Church on this reservation about 28 years ago and have lived together ever since, as man and wife.

IN TESTIMONY WHEREOF, I have set my hand and seal to this my last will and testament, at Crow Creek Agency Office, Crow Creek, South Dakota, on this 7th day of May, in the year of our Lord Nineteen hundred and fourteen.   His

Seeking Land [thumb print]

mark:

SIGNED, SEALED, PUBLISHED AND DECLARED by the said Seeking Land or Makohnihda, in our presence, as and for his last Will and Testament, and at his request and in his presence, and in the presence of each other, we have hereunto subscribed our names as attesting witnesses, the testator's name having been subscribed thereto at his request by W.C. Kohlenberg.

W.C. Kohlenberg	Residence, Crow Creek, South Dakota.
Homer J Bibb	Residence, Crow Creek, South Dakota.
George H Always	Residence, Crow Creek, South Dakota.

Department of The Interior,
Office of Indian Affairs, Washington,
OCT 5 1914

The within will is hereby recommended for approval pursuant to the provisions of the Act of June 25, 1910 (36 Stats. L., 855-6) as amended by Act of February 14, 1913 (37 Stats. L., 678).

Respectfully,
EB Meritt
Assistant Commissioner

Department of The Interior
Office of The Secretary OCT 8 1914

The within will is hereby approved pursuant to the provisions of the Act of June 25, 1910 (36 Stats. L., 855-6) as amended by Act of February 14, 1913 (37 Stats. L., 678).

Bo Sweeney
Assistant Secretary

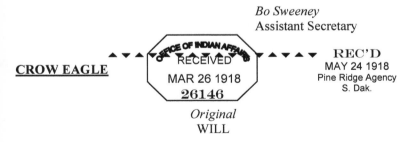

CROW EAGLE

OFFICE OF INDIAN AFFAIRS
RECEIVED
MAR 26 1918
26146

REC'D
MAY 24 1918
Pine Ridge Agency
S. Dak.

Original
WILL

I, **Crow Eagle** of Pine Ridge Agency, South Dakota, Allottee number **327** do hereby make and declare this to be my last will and testament, in accordance with Section 2 of the Act of June 25, 1910, (36 stat. 855-858) and Act of February 14, 1913, (Public No. 381), hereby revoking all former wills made by me:

1. I hereby direct that as soon as possible after my decease, that all my debts, funeral and testamentary expenses be paid out of my personal estate.

2. I give and devise my allotment on the Pine Ridge Reservation, South Dakota, described as follows:

Section 30, T 36, R 45. 640 acres.

in the following manner:

S/2 of Sec. 30, T 36, R 45, 320 acres to my wife, Bear Comes Out.

N/2 of Sec. 30, T 36, R 45, 320 acres to my nephew, Joseph Crow Eagle.

3. I give and bequeath all of my personal property of whatsoever nature and wheresoever situated unto

One wagon, one set of harness, one mare, and one gelding to my wife, Bear Comes Out.

One cow to Joseph Crow Eagle, my nephew.

4. All the rest of my property, real or personal, now possessed or hereafter acquired, of whatsoever nature and wheresoever situated, I hereby give, devise and bequeath unto

my wife, Bear Comes Out.

In witness whereof I have hereunto set my hand this **13th** day of **March** 1918   *his*
Crow Eagle [thumb print]
mark

The above statement was, this **13th** day of **March** 1918 signed and published by **Crow Eagle** as **his** last will and testament, in the joint presence of the undersigned, the said **Crow Eagle** then being of sound and vigorous mind and free from any constraint or compulsion; whereupon we, being without any interest in the matter other than friendship, and being well acquainted with **him** but not members of **his** family, immediately subscribed our names hereto in the presence of each other and of the said testator, for the purpose of attesting the said will, as **he** requested us to do. And that I, **Henry Many Cartridges** at the testator's request have written **his** name in ink, and that I affixed **his** thumb-marks.

	Post Office Address
Henry Many Cartridges	**Pine Ridge, S.D.**
John (Illegible)	**Pine Ridge, S.D.**

Pine Ridge, South Dakota.
Apr 21 1918

I hereby certify that I have fully inquired into the mental competency of the Indian signing the above will; the circumstances attending the execution of the will; the influence that may have induced its execution, and the names of those entitled to share in the estate under the law of descent in South Dakota: reasons for the disposition of the property proposed by the will differing from disposition had the property descended by operation of law.

I respectfully forward this will with the recommendation that it be …..approved.

(No Signature)
Supt. & Spl. Disb. Agent.

Department of The Interior,
Office of Indian Affairs, Washington,

The within will of Crow Eagle is hereby recommended for approval in accordance with the Act of June 25, 1910 (36 Stats. L., 855-6) as amended by Act of February 14, 1913 (37 Stats. L., 678).

Respectfully,
EB Meritt
Assistant Commissioner

Department of The Interior
Office of The Secretary MAR -6 1920

The within will is hereby approved in accordance with the provisions of the Act of June 25, 1910 (36 Stats. L., 855-6) as amended by Act of February 14, 1913 (37 Stats. L., 678).

Alexander T Vogelsburg
First Assistant Secretary

▲ ▼ ▲ ▼ ▲ ▼ ▲ ▼ ▲ ▼ ▲ ▼ ▲ ▼

WOOD-AH-CO-NY

OFFICE OF INDIAN AFFAIRS
RECEIVED
MAY 28 1917
52183

LAST WILL AND TESTAMENT

I, Wood-ah-co-ny, 68 years of age, of Walters Cotton County, Oklahoma, being now in good health, strength of body and mind, but sensible of the uncertainty of life and desiring to make disposition of my property and affairs while in health and strength, do hereby make, publish and declare the following to be my last will and testament, hereby revoking and cancelling all other and former wills by me at any time made.

1. I direct the payment of all my just debts and funeral expenses.

2. I give and devise to my beloved husband Pe-ah-coose, Comanche Indian allottee No. 1073, and to my beloved grand-daughter Com-mock, Comanche Indian allottee No. 1074, all of my property, real and personal, of which I may die possessed, including the unsold portion of my trust allotment of land comprising the Fr. W/2 of NW/4 18-28-10W, containing 70.80 acres more or less and known upon the rolls of the Interior Department as Comanche Indian allotment 1074, said Granddaughter and said husband to share equally in all of my property.

This will is made subject to the approval of the Secretary of the Interior.

In witness whereof I, Wood-ah-cony, have to this my last will and testament, consisting of two (2) sheets of paper, subscribed my name this *15th* day of *May*, 1917.

her
Wood-ah-cony [thumb print]
mark

Witnesses:
Bob Homacheet
Robert Lines

Subscribed by Wood-ah-cony in the presence of each of us the undersigned and at the same time declared by her to us to be her last will and testament and we thereupon at the request of Wood-ah-cony, in her presence and in the presence of each other, sign our names hereto as witnesses, this *15th* day of *May, 1917*, a Walters, Cotton County, Oklahoma.

Robert Lines
P.O. *Walters, Okla.*
Bob Homacheet
P.O. *Walters, Okla.*

Probate
52183-17
8966-19
W L W

Department of The Interior,
Office of Indian Affairs, Washington,
MAR -6 1920

The within will of Wood-ah-cony, deceased allottee No. 1074, is hereby recommended for approval in accordance with the provisions of the Act of June 25, 1910 (36 Stats. L., 855-6) as amended by Act of February 14, 1913 (37 Stats. L., 678).

EB Meritt
Assistant Commissioner

Department of The Interior
Office of The Secretary

Pursuant to the provisions of the Act of June 25, 1910 (36 Stats. L., 855-6) as amended by Act of February 14, 1913 (37 Stats. L., 678) and the Regulations of the Department, I hereby approve the within will of Wood-ah-cony, deceased allottee No. 1074.

SG Hopkins
ASSISTANT Secretary

▲ ▼ ▲ ▼ ▲ ▼ ▲ ▼ ▲ ▼ ▲ ▼ ▲ ▼

MARY A KEOKUK

LAST WILL AND TESTAMENT OF
Mary A. Keokuk

Indian Wills, 1911 – 1921 Book Six
Records of The Bureau of Indian Affairs

I, **Mary A. Keokuk**, being now of sound and disposing mind and memory, and being desirous of providing for the disposition of my property after my death, do now make, publish and declare this as my last will and testament, hereby revoking any and all previous wills by me made.

1. I direct the payment of all my just debts and funeral expenses.

2. I give, bequeath and devise unto **Leo Whistler** of **Sac and Fox Agency, St Paul, Oklahoma** all and singular the property of every kind of which I shall die seized, both real and personal property as recompense for his care of me in my declining years.

3. I hereby nominate **The Superintendent of the Sac and Fox Indian School, Stroud Oklahoma**, as the executor of this, my last will and testament.

Witness my hand at **Sac and Fox Agency, Stroud, Oklahoma**, this *26th* day of *February* 19*19*.

Mary A. Keokuk

Subscribed by **Mary A. Keokuk** in the presence of each of us, the undersigned, and at the same time declared by her to be her last will and testament, and we, thereupon, at her request and in her presence and in the presence of each other, sign our names hereto as witnesses, this *26th* day of *Feb* 19*19*.

| *Mary Johnson* | address | *Stroud, Okla.* |
| *F. N. Kryman* | Address | *Stroud, Okla.* |

Department of The Interior,
Office of Indian Affairs, Washington, MAR -9 1920

It is hereby recommended that the within will of Mary A. Keokuk, deceased, be approved under the provisions of the Act of June 25, 1910 (36 Stats. L., 855-6) as amended by Act of February 14, 1913 (37 Stats. L., 678), and the regulations of the Department.

Yours very truly,
EB Meritt
Assistant Commissioner

Indian Wills, 1911 – 1921 Book Six
Records of The Bureau of Indian Affairs

Department of The Interior
Office of The Secretary

The within will of Mary A. Keokuk, decease, is hereby approved under the provisions of the Act of June 25, 1910 (36 Stats. L., 855-6) as amended by Act of February 14, 1913 (37 Stats. L., 678), and the regulations of the Department.

SG Hopkins
ASSISTANT Secretary

▲▼▲▼▲▼▲▼▲▼▲▼▲▼▲▼

JOHN B. LAFAVE

I, John B. Lafave, living at No. 395 West Third Street, Superior, Wisconsin, an unmarried man, being of sound mind and memory, do make, publish and declare this my last Will and Testament, namely:

I give, devise and bequeath to my sister, Sophie Belair, all of my estate both real and personal, and I appoint her executrix of this my Will and direct that she be not required to give any bond for the faithful discharge of said trust.

I am a Chippewa half-breed and was born at LaPointe on Madaline Island and when about ten years old came to Superior with my parents and the other members of the family. We came by boat and landed at Superior August 15, 1853; so my sister Sophie and I are the oldest residents of the Head of Lake Superior. Ever since then I have lived in Superior except that a various times I have been away for periods. At one time I lived several years at the Lac Court Oreilles[sic] Indian Reservation and became entitled to a selection of land on said Reservation and this land was patented to me and is described as the West half of the North East quarter of Section Thirty-one (31) in Township Thirty-nine (39) North of Range Seven (7) West. containing 80 acres. For a number of years I have suffered from rheumatism and so crippled that I have been unable to work and since I have been have been[sic] in this disabled condition I have lived at my sister Sophie's house and she has cared for me and most kindly supplied all my wants and in gratitude to her I desire all my property to go to her.

The patent for the land spoken of above is before me. In this patent my name is wrongly written as "John La Faver," but I declare that I am the man to whom the patent issued and that I own said land according to the terms of the patent.

In Witness Whereof I have to this instrument set my hand and seal at Superior, Wisconsin, this 23rd day of November, 1915.

his
John X B. Lafave   (Seal)
mark

Signed, sealed, published and declared by the said John B. Lafave as and for his last Will and Testament in the presence of us, who, at his request in his presence and in the presence of each other, have hereunto subscribed our names as attesting witnesses.

Henry S. Butler, 466 West 3rd St., Superior, Wis.

William B. Perry, 353 West 5th St., Superior, Wis.

Department of The Interior,
Office of Indian Affairs, Washington,
JAN 28 1920
It is respectfully recommended that the within certified copy of the will of John B. Lafave, Chippewa allottee No. 534, be submitted to the President for his approval.

EB Meritt
Acting Commissioner.

Department of The Interior
Office of The Secretary FEB 12 1920

The within will of John B. Lafave is respectfully submitted for approval.

Franklin K Payne
Secretary

THE WHITE HOUSE

13 February 1920
Approved:
Woodrow Wilson

▲▼▲▼▲▼▲▼▲▼▲▼▲▼▲▼

PAH-VID-SE BALLARD

LAST WILL AND TESTAMENT

**OFFICE OF INDIAN AFFAIRS
RECEIVED
SEP 10 1919
77476**

In the name of God, Amen. I, PAH-VID-SE BALLARD, Fort Hall Allottee No. 624, of Fort Hall, County of Bingham, State of Idaho, a member of the Shoshone Tribe of Indians, being about seventy-two years of age and of sound and disposing mind and memory and sensible of the uncertainty of life, desiring to make provision for the disposition of any and all property, rights, interests and estates of which I may die seized and possessed, and not acting under duress, menace, fraud or undue influence of any person whatsoever, do hereby make, publish, and declare this, my last will and testament in manner and form as follows: that is to say:

First. I direct that all my just debts and funeral expenses shall be paid out of my estate as soon after my decease as shall be found convenient.

Second. I give and devise to my step-son, Johnny Book Ballard, the only living son of my deceased husband, Jim Ballard, the W1/2 SW1/4 SW1/4 Sec 17, T 5 S, R 36 E containing 20 acres; Lot 13, Sec. 31, T 4 S, R 36 E containing 40.51 acres; and Lots 4, 5, & 12 Sec. 6 T 5 S, R 36 E B.M. containing 119.49 acres, in all 180 acres more or less.

Third. I give, devise and bequeath to my step-son Johnny Book Ballard, the identical person names in the second provision hereof, all of my personal property to which I have title at my decease.

Fourth. I give, devise, and bequeath all other property, rights, interests and estates, of which I may die possessed or seized, or to which I may be entitled, to the said Johnny Book Ballard, Fort Hall allottee No. 625, to the exclusion of all other persons whomsoever.

Fifth. It is my intention that my step-son Johnny Book Ballard be the sole beneficiary under this my last will and testament in exclusion of all other persons whomsoever, who, otherwise, would take as my heirs at law, my action in so doing being out of regard for the care and attention given me and my deceased husband, Jim Ballard during our old age by Johnny Book Ballard and because of the fact that I have raised the said Johnny Book Ballard from childhood to manhood and felt toward him as toward my own children; and further that there is no person living who is closer or dearer to me than the said Johnny Book Ballard.

IN TESTIMONY WHEREOF, I have executed the within and foregoing instrument (2 pages only) by causing my name to be subscribed hereto by an attesting witness, and the impression by me of my thumb mark, this 6th day of September, 1918.

Her
Pah-vid-se Ballard [thumb print]
Mark

The foregoing instrument of 2 pages only was on this 6th day of September, 1918, executed by Pah-vid-se Ballard by herself causing her name to be subscribed thereto by L.G. Kendrick and by the impression of the thumb mark of Pah-vid-se Ballard by herself thereon set, in the presence of us, and at the time of her subscribing said instrument she declared it to be her last will and testament, and at her request and in her presence, and in the presence of each other, we subscribe our names as witnesses, with ou[sic] respective places of residence, the day and year lat above written.

Witnesses:

L G Kendrick
Fort Hall, Idaho.
Aletha Hardy
Fort Hall, Idaho.

Joseph Rainey, being duly sworn, on his oath declares, that he acted as interpreter, and fully and correctly interpreted all the above and foregoing to Pah-vid-se Ballard, and is satisfied that she understands it and was fully qualified to execute the same.

Joseph Rainey
Interpreter

Subscribed and sworn to before me this 6th day of September 1918.

Le C Hardy
Notary Public.

Department of The Interior,
Office of Indian Affairs, Washington,
MAR 15 1920

The within will of Pahvidse Ballard, deceased allottee No. 624, of the Bannock tribe, is respectfully recommended for approval pursuant to the provisions of the Act of June 25, 1910 (36 Stats. L., 855-6) as amended by Act of February 14, 1913 (37 Stats. L., 678).

> *EB Meritt*
> Assistant Commissioner

Department of The Interior
Office of The Secretary MAR 15 1920

The within will of Pahvidse Ballard, deceased allottee No. 624, of the Bannock tribe, is hereby approved pursuant to the provisions of the Act of June 25, 1910 (36 Stats. L., 855-6) as amended by Act of February 14, 1913 (37 Stats. L., 678), and it is found and held that the testatrix's stepson, Johnny Book Ballard, inherits the entire estate as sole devisee.

> *SG Hopkins*
> ASSISTANT Secretary

OFFICE OF INDIAN AFFAIRS
RECEIVED
JAN 22, 1919
6443

HENRY MARTIN or KE-KIG-KUM

LAST WILL AND TESTAMENT OF HENRY MARTIN.

I, Henry Martin of Nisqually Tribe of Indians, Nisqually Reservation, Cushman Agency, Washington, of the age of upwards of 80 years, and being of sound and disposing mind and memory, and not acting under duress, menace, fraud, or undue influence of any person whatever, do make, publish, and declare this MY LAST WILL AND TESTAMENT, in the manner following, that is to say:

FIRST, for and in the consideration of personal care and a comfortable home for the last seven years and the continuation thereof for the remainder of my lifetime, I do give, devise and bequeath to PETER KALAMA, my nephew, that tract of land on the Nisqually Reservation, inherited by me from the estate of Qualamuth or Robert, Nisqually Allottee No. 24, (Law 72667-1912, Dec. 23, 1912), described as Lots 8, 9, 10, 11, 12 & 13, Sec. 34, and Lot 10, Sec 35, all in Twp. 18 N. Range 1

E.W.M, Washington, 132.46 acres.

SECOND, I hereby revoke all former wills.

In witness whereof, I have hereunto set my hand and seal this 18th day of October, 1917.

his thumb
Henry Martin [thumb print]
mark

WITNESSES TO THUMB MARK:
O.H. Keller, Chief Clerk
Tacoma Wash.
M.M. Longonlaugh, Clerk
Tacoma, Wash.

The above and foregoing instrument was, at the date thereof, signed and sealed by the said Henry Martin, and published as and declared to be his last will and testament in the presence of us, who, at his request and in his presence, and in the presence of each other, have subscribed our names as witnesses thereto.

O.H. Keller
(Signature Illegible)

Department of The Interior,
Office of Indian Affairs, Washington,
FEB -2 1910

It is respectfully recommended that the within will of Henry Martin or Ke-kig-kum, Nisqually allottee 23, be submitted to the President for his approval.

EB Meritt
Assistant Commissioner.

Department of The Interior
Office of The Secretary   FEB 17 1920

The within will of Henry Martin or Ke-kig-kum, Nisqually allottee 23, is respectfully submitted for approval.

Franklin K Payne
Secretary

THE WHITE HOUSE
17 February 1920
Approved:
Woodrow Wilson

▲▼▲▼▲▼▲▼▲▼▲▼▲▼▲▼

NICK-E-ZIK-AH

OFFICE OF INDIAN AFFAIRS
RECEIVED
JUN 17 1919
51404

LAST WILL AND TESTAMENT

In the name of God, Amen. I, Nick-e-zik-ah, Fort Hall Allottee No. 772, of Fort Hall, County of Bingham, State of Idaho, a member of the Shoshone Tribe of Indians, being about eighty-eight years of age and of sound and disposing mind and memory and sensible of the uncertainty of life, desiring to make provision for the disposition of any and all property, rights, interests and estates of which I may die seized and possessed, and not acting under duress, menace or fraud or undue influence of any person whatsoever, do hereby make, publish and declare this, my last will and testament in manner and form as follows: that is to say:

First: I direct that all my just debts and funeral expenses shall be paid out of my estate as soon after my decease as shall be found convenient.

Second: I give and devise to my son Billy George, Fort Hall Allottee No. 763, my allotment on the Fort Hall Indian Reservation, in the State of Idaho. described as the E1/2 SE1/4 SE1/4 Section 30, and the NE1/4 Section 32, Township 3 south, Range 35 East Boise Meridian, Idaho, containing 180 acres, more or less.

Third: I give and devise to my son Billy George, Fort Hall Allottee No. 763, all other property both real and personal, which I may die possessed, and not otherwise bequeathed in this my last will and testament.

In witness whereof, I have executed the within and foregoing instrument (1 page only) by causing my name to be subscribed hereto by an attesting witness, and the impression by me of my thumb mark, this 3rd day of May, 1918.

His

Witnesses to Mark.　　　　　　　　Nick-e-zik-ah [thumb print] mark
　　Lee C. Hardy
　　Joseph Rainey

Department of The Interior,
Office of Indian Affairs, Washington,
MAR 13 1920

Indian Wills, 1911 – 1921 Book Six
Records of The Bureau of Indian Affairs

The within will of Nickezikah, deceased allottee No. 772 of the Shoshone tribe, is respectfully recommended for approval pursuant to the provisions of the Act of June 25, 1910 (36 Stats. L., 855-6) as amended by Act of February 14, 1913 (37 Stats. L., 678).

EB Meritt
Assistant Commissioner

Department of The Interior
Office of The Secretary   JAN 14 1921

The within will of Nickezikah, deceased allottee No. 772 of the Shoshone tribe, is hereby approved pursuant to the provisions of the Act of June 25, 1910 (36 Stats. L., 855-6) as amended by Act of February 14, 1913 (37 Stats. L., 678), and it is found and held that the testator's son, Billy George, inherits the entire estate as sole devisee.

SG Hopkins
ASSISTANT Secretary

IMITATES CHEYENNE

OFFICE OF INDIAN AFFAIRS
RECEIVED
MAR 29 1920
26832

Original
WILL

OFFICE OF INDIAN AFFAIRS
RECEIVED
SEP 26 1914
103829

I, **Imitates Cheyenne** of Pine Ridge Agency, South Dakota, Allottee number **1481** do hereby make and declare this to be my last will and testament, in accordance with Section 2 of the Act of June 25, 1910, (36 stat. 855-858) and Act of February 14, 1913, (Public No. 381), hereby revoking all former wills made by me:

1. I hereby direct that as soon as possible after my decease, that all my debts, funeral and testamentary expenses be paid out of my personal estate.

2. I give and devise my allotment on the Pine Ridge Reservation, South Dakota, described as follows:

The N/2 of S/2 of Sec. 25 in Twp. 40 N. of Range 41 west of the 6th P.M., and the S/2 of Sec. 30 and the NE/4 of Sec. 19 in Twp. 40 north of Range 40 west of the Sixth Principal Meridian, South Dakota, containing 540 acres.

in the following manner:

To my wife Gives Things, my grand-daughter, Mary Ruff, my friends, George Two Crow and Prairie Dog: The N/2 of S/2 of Sec. 25 in Twp. 40 N. of Range 41 and the NE/4 of Sec. 19 in Twp. 40 N of Range 40 west of the 6th P.M.

The S/2 of Sec. 30 in Twp. 40 N of Range 40 west of the 6th P.M., I wish to sell and use the money for my support. Should there be any money remaining I wish for my wife, Gives Things to have same. Should the land not sell, I wish for my wife, Give Things, to have this half-section.

3. I give and bequeath all of my personal property of whatsoever nature and wheresoever situated unto

To my wife, Gives Things.

4. All the rest of my property, real or personal, now possessed or hereafter acquired, of whatsoever nature and wheresoever situated, I hereby give, devise and bequeath unto

To my wife, Gives Things.

In witness whereof I have hereunto set my hand this **12th** day of **August 1914.**

his mark[thumb print]
Imitates Cheyenne

The above statement was, this **12th** day of **August** 1914 signed and published by **Imitates Cheyenne** as **his** last will and testament, in the joint presence of the undersigned, the said **Imitates Cheyenne** then being of sound and vigorous mind and free from any constraint or compulsion; whereupon we, being without any interest in the matter other than friendship, and being well acquainted with **him** but not members of **his** family, immediately subscribed our names hereto in the presence of each other and of the said testator, for the purpose of attesting the said will, as **he** requested us to do, **his name being signed by George A. Trotter, one of the witnesses, at his request.**

Post Office Address

George A Trotter **Kyle, South Dakota.**

Hugh Top Bear **Kyle, South Dakota.**

Pine Ridge, South Dakota.

SEP 22 1914

I hereby certify that I have fully inquired into the mental competency of the Indian signing the above will; the circumstances attending the execution of the will; the influence that may have induced its execution, and the names of those entitled to share in the estate under the law of descent in South Dakota: reasons for the disposition of the property proposed by the will differing from disposition had the property descended by operation of law.

I respectfully forward this will with the recommendation that it be …..approved.

John R Brennan
Supt. & Spl. Disb. Agent.

Department of The Interior,
Office of Indian Affairs, Washington,

NOV 18 1914

The within will of Imitates Cheyenne, is recommended for approval in accordance with the Act of June 25, 1910 (36 Stats. L., 855-6) as amended by Act of February 14, 1913 (37 Stats. L., 678).

EB Meritt
Assistant Commissioner

Department of The Interior
Office of The Secretary NOV 25 1914

The within will of Imitates Cheyenne, is approved in accordance with the Act of June 25, 1910 (36 Stats. L., 855-6) as amended by Act of February 14, 1913 (37 Stats. L., 678).

Bo Sweeney
Assistant Secretary

TA-NE-TANE

Last Will and Testament

OFFICE OF INDIAN AFFAIRS
RECEIVED
AUG 18 1917
78611

80

Indian Wills, 1911 – 1921 Book Six
Records of The Bureau of Indian Affairs

I, Ta-ne-tane Kiowa Indian allottee No. 1394, sound in mind and body, but conscious of the uncertainty of life, and desiring to make disposition of my property and affairs while in health and strength, do hereby make, publish, and declare the following to be my last will and testament, hereby revoking and cancelling all other and former wills by me at any time made.

First: I direct the payment of all my just debts and funeral expenses.

Second: I give and devise to my beloved daughter, A-sane-hiddle, Kiowa Indian allottee No. 1424, all of my interest in and to the South West Quarter of Section thirty-three (33) Township six, North (6N) of Range thirteen (13) West of the Indian Meridian, in Oklahoma, known upon the rolls of the Interior Department as Kiowa Indian allotment No. 1395, Pan-tang-ke, deceased allottee. In decree of the Department "L.H. 56347-15 F.E." I was declared to be an heir in and to said allotment to the extent of one-third thereof.

Third: I give and devise to my beloved son To-paum, Kiowa Indian allottee No. 1396, the sum of One Hundred ($100.$^{\underline{00}}$) Dollars, to be paid by the Officers of the Kiowa Indian Agency from any funds remaining to my credit after my death.

Fourth: I give and bequeath all the rest, residue and remainder of my property real and personal to my beloved daughter, A-sane-hiddle, Kiowa Indian allottee 1424.

In witness whereof, I, Ta-ne-tane, have hereunto set my name this 4th day of August, A.D. 1916,to this my last will and testament, consisting of four pages of paper.

his thumb
Ta-ne-tane [thumb print]
mark

Witnesses
H.E. Bretschneider
Jasper Saunkeah
Anadarko, Okla.

We, the undersigned t the request of Ta-ne-tane, who subscribed the foregoing in our presence and in the presence of each other, at the same time declaring to us that the foregoing constituted his last will and testament, have hereunto set our names as witnesses, in the presence of

81

Ta-ne-tane and in the presence of each other, this 4th day of August, A.D. 1916, near Carnagie, Oklahoma.

> *H.E. Bretschneider*
> *Anadarko, Okla.*
> *Jasper Saunkeah*
> *Anadarko, Okla.*

I, Jasper Saunkeah, hereby certify on honor that I acted as interpreter during the execution of the foregoing will by Ta-ne-tane; that this will was drawn strictly in accordance with his desires and directions and that I have no interest in this matter. That I speak both the Kiowa Indian as well as the English languages fluently.

Signed this 4th day of August, 1916.

> *Jasper Saunkeah*
> *Interpreter*

Department of The Interior,
Office of Indian Affairs, Washington, MAR 16 1920

It is recommended that the within will of Ta-ne-tane, Kiowa Indian allottee No. 1394, be approved in accordance with the provisions of the Act of June 25, 1910 (36 Stats. L., 855-6) as amended by Act of February 14, 1913 (37 Stats. L., 678).

> Respectfully,
> *EB Meritt*
> Assistant Commissioner

Department of The Interior
Office of The Secretary

The within will of Ta-ne-tane, Kiowa Indian allottee No. 1394, is hereby approved in accordance with the provisions of the Act of June 25, 1910 (36 Stats. L., 855-6) as amended by Act of February 14, 1913 (37 Stats. L., 678).

> *SG Hopkins*
> ASSISTANT Secretary

▲▼▲▼▲▼▲▼▲▼▲▼▲▼

POOR DOG *his mark*
[thumb print]

LAST WILL AND TESTAMENT

IN THE NAME OF GOD, AMEN. I, *Poor Dog* of *Rosebud* in the County of *Todd* and State of *So Dak*, being of sound mind and memory, and considering the uncertainty of this frail and transitory life, do therefore make, ordain, publish and declare this to be my Last Will and Testament.

First, I order and direct that my execut hereinafter named, pay all my just debts and funeral expenses as soon after my decease as conveniently may be.

Second, After the payment of such funeral expenses and debts, I give, devise and bequeath: *to Nannie Dorine Bordedux the following SW1/4 of Sec. 5, R 30, T 35*
and to
Joseph Poor Dog the SE1/4 of Sec. 5, R 30, T 35
SW1/4 of Sec. 7, R 30, T. 35
SE1/4 of Sec. 7, R 30, T. 35

Lastly, I make, constitute and appoint the Superintendent of the Rosebud Indian Agency, Executor of this, my Last Will and Testament, hereby revoking all former Wills by me made.

IN TESTIMONY WHEREOF, I have hereunto subscribed my name and affixed my seal the *(Blank)* day of *(Blank)* in the year of our Lord One Thousand nine Hundred *(Blank)* .

(Testator's thumb print at the top of Will)

THIS INSTRUMENT was, on the day of the date thereof, signed, published and declared by said testator*(Blank)* to be h*(Blank)* Last Will and Testament, in our presence, who, at h*(Blank)* request, have subscribed our names hereto as witnesses, in h*(Blank)* presence, and in the presence of each other.

M.L. McIntyre	residing at	*St. Francis, S.D.*
P. F. Digman	residing at	*St. Francis, S.D.*

Department of The Interior,
Office of Indian Affairs, Washington,

It is recommended that the within will be approved pursuant to the provisions of the Act of June 25, 1910 (36 Stats. L., 855-6) as amended by Act of February 14, 1913 (37 Stats. L., 678).

> Respectfully,
> *EB Meritt*
> Assistant Commissioner

Department of The Interior
Office of The Secretary

MAR 30 1920

The within will is hereby approved pursuant to the provisions of the Act of June 25, 1910 (36 Stats. L., 855-6) as amended by Act of February 14, 1913 (37 Stats. L., 678).

> *SG Hopkins*
> Assistant Secretary

▲▼▲▼▲▼▲▼▲▼▲▼▲▼

A-GOPE-TAH

> OFFICE OF INDIAN AFFAIRS
> RECEIVED
> JUN 19 1917
> **59693**

LAST WILL AND TESTAMENT

> Carnegie, Okla.
> *April 18,* 1917.

I, A-gope-tah, Kiowa Indian allottee No. 475, at Carnegie, Caddo County, Oklahoma, sound in body and mind, but sensible of the uncertainty of life and desiring to make disposition of my personal property and affairs while in health and strength, do hereby make, publish and declare the following to be my last will and testament, hereby revoking and cancelling all other and former wills by me at any time made.

First I direct the payment of all my just debts and funeral expenses.

Second, I direct that my allotment of land, comprising the NW/4, Sec. 27, Twp. 7N, R 8 W, of the I.M., in Oklahoma, known upon the rolls of the Interior Department as Kiowa Allotment 275, be partitioned by order of the Secretary of the Interior in the following manner:

a.   That the NE/4 of the NW/4-27-7N-8, be granted to my beloved son, Tah-do (William Bird A-gope-tah), Kiowa Indian Allottee No. 277.

84

b.   That the SE/4 of said NW/4-27-7N-8, be granted to my beloved daughter Au-koy (Maggie Jackson), Kiowa Indian Allottee No. 22.

c.   That the SW/4 of said NW/4-27-7N-8, be granted to my beloved daughter Tine-goo-ah, Kiowa Indian allottee No. 614, who is otherwise knows as Susie Cat.

d.   That the NW/4 of said NW/4-27-7N-8, be granted to my beloved grand children Tsodle-man (Sadie Aunko), Kiowa Indian No. 609, and Paddle-tso (John Aunko), Kiowa Indian Allottee No. 608. These two last named beneficiaries are brother and sister and I desire and direct that they have each an undivided 1/2 interest in and to said NW/4 of NW/4-27-7N-8.

I have no husband and these are my sole heirs at law and this is my declaration to that effect.

I give and bequeath all the rest, residue and remainder of my property, real and personal, of which I may die possessed to the following persons in the shares named:

1.   To my beloved son, Tah-do (William Bird A-go-e-tah), Kiowa Indian allottee No. 277, ... 1/4

2.   To my beloved daughter Au-ko (Maggie Jackson), Kiowa Indian allottee No. 22, ... 1/4

3.   To my beloved daughter, Tine-goo-ah (Susie Cat) Kiowa Indian allottee No. 614, ... 1/4

4.   To my beloved grandson Paddle-tso (John Aunko) Kiowa Indian allottee No. 608, ... 1/8

5.   To my beloved granddaughter Tsodle-man (Sadie Aunko) Kiowa Indian allottee No. 609, ... 1/8

This will is made subject to the approval of the Secretary of the Interior.

In witness whereof I, A-gope-tah, have to this my last will and testament, consisting of three (3) sheets of paper, subscribed my name this *18* day of *April* 1917.

A-gope-tah   [thumb print]

Witnesses:
Claude Brown
John A. Law

Subscribed by A-gope-tah, in the presence of each of us the undersigned and at the same time declared by her to us to be her last will and testament and we thereupon at the request of A-gope-tah, in her presence and in the presence of each other, sign our names hereto as witnesses, this *18* day of *April*, 1917, at *Carnegie, Okla,* Oklahoma.

Claude Brown
Carnegie, Okla.
Post Office
John A. Law
Carnegie, Okla.
Post Office
Dist. Farmer #2

Department of The Interior,
Office of Indian Affairs, Washington,

MAR -9 1920

It is hereby recommended that the within will of A-gope-tah, Kiowa Indian allottee No. 475, be approved under the provisions of the Act of June 25, 1910 (36 Stats. L., 855-6) as amended by Act of February 14, 1913 (37 Stats. L., 678), and the regulations of the Department.

Respectfully,
EB Meritt
Assistant Commissioner

Department of The Interior
Office of The Secretary   MAR 24 1920

The within will of A-gope-tah, Kiowa Indian allottee No. 475, is hereby approved under the provisions of the Act of June 25, 1910 (36 Stats. L., 855-6) as amended by Act of February 14, 1913 (37 Stats. L., 678), and the regulations of the Department.

SG Hopkins
Assistant Secretary

▲ ▼ ▲ ▼ ▲ ▼ ▲ ▼ ▲ ▼ ▲ ▼ ▲ ▼

EAGLE

Last Will and Testament
of
Eagle, Wife of Gros Ventre No 1

IN THE NAME OF GOD, AMEN.

I, *Eagle, Wife of Gros Ventre No 1* of *Wyola Mont* being of sound mind, memory, and understanding, do hereby make and publish this my last will and testament, hereby revoking and annulling all wills by me heretofore made, in manner and form following, that is to say:

First; I direct that all my just debts and funeral expenses, and expenses of my last illness shall be paid by my executor hereinafter named as soon after my decease as convenient;
Second; I give, devise and bequeath to

My husband Gros Ventre No (1)
One half of all my property both real and personal

and to my adopted daughter Annie Hill
one half of all my property both real and personal

Third; All the rest and residue of my estate, both real, and personal and mixed, I give devise and bequeath to my lawful heirs as determined after my decease.
And lastly; I do hereby nominate, constitute and appoint *Supt Evan W Aslep or his successor* executor of this my last will and testament.
In testimony Whereof, I have set my hand and seal to this, my last will and Testament, at *Lodge Grass* Montana, this *28th* day of *December*, in the year of our Lord one thousand nine hundred and *Sixteen*.   *Her*

Eagle [thumb print]
mark.

Signed, sealed, published and declared by said *Eagle* in our presence, as and for *her* last Will and testament, and at *her* request and in our presence, and in the presence of each other, we have hereunto subscribed our names as attesting witnesses thereto.

SP Cooper	of	***Lodge Grass, Mont.***
George Hill	of	***Lodge Grass, Mont***
Blake White Bear	of	***Lodge Grass, Mont***

Department of The Interior,
Office of Indian Affairs, Washington,
APR -7 1920

The within proposed will of Eagle, deceased Crow allottee, No. 1388, signed December 28, 1916, is respectfully recommended for approval in accordance with the provisions of the Act of June 25, 1910 (36 Stats. L., 855-6) as amended by Act of February 14, 1913 (37 Stats. L., 678).

Respectfully,
EB Meritt
Assistant Commissioner

Department of The Interior
Office of The Secretary

The within proposed will of Eagle, deceased Crow allottee, No. 1388, signed December 28, 1916, is hereby approved under the Act of June 25, 1910 (36 Stats. L., 855-6) as amended by Act of February 14, 1913 (37 Stats. L., 678). he designation of an executor is not recognized.

SG Hopkins
Assistant Secretary

RECEIVED
NOV 8- 1919
96124

THERESE OCEAN

In the name of God, Amen. I, THERESE OCEAN, Fort Hall Allottee No. 1161, of Fort Hall, County of Bingham, State of Idaho, a member of the Bannock Tribe of Indians, being about seventy years of age and of sound and disposing mind and memory, and sensible of the uncertainty of life, desiring to make provision[sic] for the disposition of any and all property, rights, interests and estates of which I may die seized and possessed, and not acting under duress, menace, fraud or undue influence of any person whatsoever, do hereby make, publish, and declare this, my last will and testament, in manner and form as follows, that is to say:

First: I direct that all my just debts and funeral expenses shall be paid out of my estate as soon after my decease as shall be found convenient.

Second: I give and devise to my niece, Malina Edmo, Fort Hall Allottee No. 503, and 52 years of age, the W1/2 of the NW1/4 of the SW1/4 of Section 16, and NE1/4 of the SW1/4 and the E1/2 of the NW1/4 of the SW1/4 of Section 16, and the W1/2 of the NE1/4 of the NW1/4 and the W1/2 of the NW1/4 of Section 20, all in Township 5 South, Range 36 East, Boise Meridian, containing 180 acres, more or less.

Third: I give, devise and bequeath to my niece Malina Edmo, the identical person named in the second provision, all my personal property consisting of the following:

Two horses and one set of harness, and any and all other personal property owned by me at my death.

Fourth: I give, devise and bequeath all other property, rights, interests and estates, of whatsoever kind or nature and wheresoever situated, of which I may die possessed of seized, or to which I may be entitled, to the said Malina Edmo, Fort Hall allottee No. 503, to the exclusion of all other persons whomsoever.

Fifth: It is my intention that my niece Malina Edmo be the sole beneficiary under this my last will and testament in exclusion of all other persons whomsoever, who, otherwise would take as my heirs at law, my action in so doing being out of regard for the care and attention given me during my old age by Malina Edmo, and the lack of care and interest displayed by all my other relatives and those who might claim as my heirs at law.

In witness whereof, I have executed the within and foregoing instrument, consisting of two pages only, by causing my name to be subscribed hereto by an attesting witness, and the impression by me of my thumb mark, this 9th day of April, 1917.

Her

Therese Ocean [thumb print]

Mark

The foregoing instrument of 2 pages only was on this 9th day of April, 1917, executed by Therese Ocean by herself causing her name to be subscribed thereto by Anna I. Brownlee and by the impression of the thumb mark of Therese Ocean by herself thereon set, in the presence of each of us, and at the time of her subscribing said instrument she declared it to be her last will and testament, and at her request and in her presence, and in the presence of each other, we subscribe our names as witnesses, with our respective places of residence, the day and year last above written.

Witnesses:

A.I. Brownlee	residing at	*Fort Hall, Ida.*
Aletha Hardy	" "	" " "

Nelson Bartlett, being duly sworn, on his oath declares, that he acted as interpreter, and fully and correctly interpreted all the above and foregoing to Therese Ocean, and am satisfied that she understood and was fully qualified to execute the same.

Nelson Bartlett

Interpreter.

Subscribed and sworn to before me this **9th** day of April, 1917.

Lee C Hardy

Notary Public

My Commission Expires Dec. 19, 1921.

Department of The Interior,
Office of Indian Affairs, Washington,

MAR 30 1920

The within will of Theresa[sic] Ocean, deceased allottee No. 1161, of the Bannock tribe, is respectfully recommended for approval pursuant to the provisions of the Act of June 25, 1910 (36 Stats. L., 855-6) as amended by Act of February 14, 1913 (37 Stats. L., 678).

EB Meritt

Assistant Commissioner

Department of The Interior
Office of The Secretary APR 12 1920

The within will of Theresa[sic] Ocean, deceased allottee No. 1161, of the Bannock tribe, is hereby approved pursuant to the provisions of the Act of June 25, 1910 (36 Stats. L., 855-6) as amended by Act of February 14, 1913 (37 Stats. L., 678) and it is found and held that the testatrix's niece, Malina Edmo, inherits the estate as sole devisee.

In view of a defective description of property in the will, it is interpreted to devise the entire estate.

SG Hopkins
ASSISTANT Secretary

▲▼▲▼▲▼▲▼▲▼▲▼▲▼▲▼

MRS. AARON GREYHAIR

W I L L.

I, Mrs. Aaron Greyhair, of the Winnebago reservation, living near Winnebago, in the county of Thurston, State of Nebraska, do hereby make, publish, and declare this my last will and testament in words and figures following:

I hereby give, devise and bequeath unto my son, James Greyhair one third part of my interest in the following described lands allotted to my deceased husband, Aaron Greyhair:-- The East half of the Southeast quarter of section eight, in township twenty six, range eight, and the northwest quarter of the southwest quarter of section fifteen, township twenty six, range nine, all in Thurston County, Nebraska.

I hereby give, devise, and bequeath unto Agnes Greyhair, the daughter of my deceased son, Lewis Joseph Geryhair, a one third part of my interest in the above described lands.

I hereby give, devise, and bequeath unto Louisa Greyhair, the daughter of my deceased son, John Greyhair, the remaining one third part of my interest in the above described lands.

I hereby give, devise and bequeath unto the said James Greyhair, Agnes Geryhair, and Louisa Greyhair, share and share alike, all interest, right, and title that I may have in the following described lands allotted to Henry C. Rice:

The Southwest quarter of the southeast quarter of section one, in township twenty six, range seven, and the southwest quarter of the northeast quarter of section thirty five, in township twenty seven, in range nine, all in Thurston County, Nebraska.

I hereby give, devise, and bequeath unto the said James Greyhair, Agnes Geryhair, and Louisa Greyhair, share and share alike, the residue of my estate, both real and personal.

Dated at Winnebago, in said Thurston County, Nebraska, this 27th day of May, (1916), in the year of our Lord one thousand nine hundred and sixteen.

Her thumb

Mrs. Aaron Greyhair [thumb print]
Mrs. Aaron Greyhair mark.

We whose names are hereunto subscribed do hereby certify that Mrs. Aaron Greyhair, the testatrix, subscribed her thumb mark to this instrument in our presence, and in the presence of each of us, and declared at the same time, in our presence and hearing, that this instrument was her last will and testament, and we, at her request, sign our names hereto in her presence as witnesses. We certify further that said instrument was duly and fully interpreted to her in our presence, and in the presence of each of us.

Frank White
Thomas Caramony
Grover Mallory

State of Nebraska, Thurston County. ss.

Mrs. Aaron Greyhair having first been duly sworn, on oath, deposes and says that she executed the foregoing will, as testatrix, that in the making of said will she has purposely omitted to give and devise any property to Isaac Greyhair and Henry Greyhair, and Cordelia Greyhair, the children of her deceased sons, John and Joseph, because said omitted children have not shown any interest, love and attention towards testatrix, whereas the said Agnes James, and Louisa have taken good care of her in many times of sickness, and have been very attentive and devoted. Further affiant sayeth not.

thumb

Mrs. Greyhair [thumb print]
mark

Subscribed in my presence and sworn to before me this 27th day of May, 1916.

A.M. Smith
Notary Public

State of Nebraska, Thurston County. SS.

Grover Mallery having first been duly sworn, on his oath, deposes and says that he has well and truly interpreted the foregoing last will and testament of the said Mrs. Aaron Greyhair to the said Mrs. Greyhair, and that he has also well and truly interpreted the foregoing affidavit of reasons why the said Mrs. Aaron Greyhair is not giving and devising any of her property to the said Henry Greyhair, Issac Greyhair, and Cordelia Greyhair, -- to the testatrix, and that the said Mrs. Aaron Greyhair knows and understands the contents of said will and testament, and that the said will and testament of Mrs. Aaron Greyhair was read to the said Mrs. Greyhair in the presence of Frank White and Thomas Caramony, and read by them.

Grover Mallery

Subscribed in my presnce[sic] and sworn to before me this 27th day of May, 1916.

A.M. Smith
Notary Public.

Department of The Interior,
Office of Indian Affairs, Washington,

The within will of Mrs. Aaron Greyhair is submitted for approval in accordance with the provisions of the Act of June 25, 1910 (36 Stats. L., 855-6) as amended by Act of February 14, 1913 (37 Stats. L., 678).

Respectfully,
EB Meritt
Assistant Commissioner

Department of The Interior
Office of The Secretary APR 14 1920

The within will of Mrs. Aaron Greyhair, an unallotted Winnebago Indian, is approved in accordance with the Act of June 25, 1910 (36 Stats. L., 855-6) as amended by Act of February 14, 1913 (37 Stats. L., 678).

93

SG Hopkins
Assistant Secretary

▲▼▲▼▲▼▲▼▲▼▲▼▲▼

RECEIVED
NOV 17 1917
106130

JULIA MOSQUITO

LAST WILL AND TESTAMENT OF JULIA MOSQUITO

* *

IN THE NAME OF GOD, AMEN:

I, Julia Mosquito, of the state of South Dakota, County of Charles Mix, being of sound and disposing mind and memory, but being uncertain of life and certain of the approach of death, and desiring to dispose of all my worldly possessions while I still have the power to do so, do make and declare this to be my last Will and Testament hereby revoking and annulling any and all Wills heretofore made by me.

1.   I bequeath to Rosa Rockboy, whom I raised from a child two years of age, the unsold portion of my allotment held in trust for me by the United States situated in Charles Mix County, South Dakota and described as follows: The W/2 of the SW/4 of the NE/4 of Section 19, in Township 94, North of Range 64, containing 20 acres and the SW/4 of the NE/4 of Section 25, in Township 94 North of Range 64, containing 40 acres. Also my undivided one-half interest. See Law Heirship 39326-15 in the estate of my deceased husband John Mosquito, consisting of Allotment #1469, located in Charles Mix County, South Dakota, and described as follows: South/2 of the SE/4 of Section 24, in Township 94 North of Range 64, comprising 80 acres, and the N/2 of the NE/4 of Section 25 in Township 94 North of Range 64, comprising 80 acres.

2.   I bequeath to my legal heirs, who are my brothers, Ironbear, Big Bear, and Pants, all the residue of my estate of whatever nature, including any inherited interest I may have other than the one mentioned above, and including any money I may have on deposit with the Superintendent of the Yankton Indian Agency after all the expenses of my last sickness and burial have been paid, and the erection of a monument to my grave to cost not more than $200.00, nor less than $150.00. Said heirs to share equally.

3. I bequeath to Rosa Rockboy, my household furniture and personal effects belonging in the house where I am now living.

IN TESTIMONY WHEREOF, I have set my hand and seal this **26th** day of **February** 1916, at Greenwood, S.D. Charles Mix County, S.D.

	her
Witnesses to mark:	Julia Mosquito [thumb print]
Louis Skunk	mark
Geo. Rock Boy	

Signed, sealed, published and declared this **26th Day of Feb** 1916 by the said Julia Mosquito, in our presence, as and for her last Will and Testament, and at her request, and in her presence, and in the presence of each other, we have hereunto subscribed our names as attesting witnesses.

Geo. Rock Boy
Louis Skunk

Department of The Interior,
Office of Indian Affairs, Washington,
APR 16 1920

It is recommended that the within will of Julia Mosquito, Yankton Sioux allottee No. 780, be approved in accordance with the provisions of the Act of June 25, 1910 (36 Stats. L., 855-6) as amended by Act of February 14, 1913 (37 Stats. L., 678).

Respectfully,
EB Meritt
Assistant Commissioner

Department of The Interior
Office of The Secretary
APR 19 1920

The within will Julia Mosquito, Yankton Sioux allottee No. 780, is approved pursuant to the provisions of the Act of June 25, 1910 (36 Stats. L., 855-6) as amended by Act of February 14, 1913 (37 Stats. L., 678).

SG Hopkins
Assistant Secretary

▲▼▲▼▲▼▲▼▲▼▲▼▲▼

SHAKING HERSELF

Indian Wills, 1911 – 1921 Book Six
Records of The Bureau of Indian Affairs

KNOW ALL MEN BY THESE PRESENTS, That I, Shaking Herself, wife of White Wolf, being of sound mind, but of poor health of body, and being desirous of making disposition of my allotment, and other worldly affairs, make this my last will and testament, revoking all former wills by me made:

I hereby give and bequeath to my daughter, Grace Whitewolf, the South half of my allotment.

I hereby give and bequeath to Eva Roman Nose, my granddaughter, the North Half of my allotment.

My allotment being the Northeast quarter of Section twenty-five in township fourteen North of Range thirteen, West of the Indian Meridian, Blaine County, State of Oklahoma.

I further request that this will be approved by the proper government officials, that it may be put into force and effect.

Witness my signature by make this 9th day of October, 1918, at Camp of Bird Seward, and I request Fenton Antelope and Bird Seward, who have interpreted this will to me, to write my name and witness my mark, and to witness this my will.

Her
Shaking Herself [thumb print]
Mark.

Witness who wrote name of
Shaking Herself:
    Fenton Antelope

Witness to mark:
    Bird Seward

We hereby certify that at the request of Shaking Herself and in her presence, we interpreted the foregoing will to Shaking Herself, and that she understood the same, and at the same time and place she declared the foregoing to be her last will and testament, and requested each of us to sign the same as witnesses, which we did in her presence and in the presence of each other.

Bird Seward	Geary, Okla. R.5
Fenton Antelope	Thomas, Okla. R.A.

I, husband of Shaking Herself, approve the foregoing will and request its approval:

His

White Wolf [thumb mark]

Witness who wrote name: Mark.

Bird Seward

Department of The Interior,
Office of Indian Affairs, Washington,

APR 17 1920

It is recommended that the within will of Shaking Herself be approved in accordance with the provisions of the Act of June 25, 1910 (36 Stats. L., 855-6) as amended by Act of February 14, 1913 (37 Stats. L., 678), and the Regulations of the Department.

Respectfully,

EB Meritt

Assistant Commissioner

Department of The Interior
Office of The Secretary   APR 22 1920

The within will Shaking Herself is hereby approved in accordance with the provisions of the Act of June 25, 1910 (36 Stats. L., 855-6) as amended by Act of February 14, 1913 (37 Stats. L., 678), and the Regulations of the Department.

SG Hopkins

Assistant Secretary

▲▼▲▼▲▼▲▼▲▼▲▼▲

MAGGIE REED

OFFICE OF INDIAN AFFAIRS
RECEIVED
APR 3- 1920
28667

WILL OF MAGGIE REED

Uintah Ute Allottee, No. 436, Uintah and Ouray Indian Reservation, Utah.

Uintah and Ouray Indian Agency, Fort Duchesne, Utah.
April 14, 1913.

KNOW ALL MEN BY THE PRESENTS, That I, <u>Maggie Reed</u>, being of sound mind and memory, do make and declare the following to be my last will and testament:-

I hereby devise and bequeath to my son, Charles E. Reed, all my personal property of every description, which I may own at the time of my death.

I hereby devise to my son aforesaid, Charles E. Reed, my allotment on the Uintah and Ouray Indian Reservation in Utah, described as follows:- The N.W.1/2 of the S.W.1/4, Section 25, Township 2 North, Range 1 West, containing 40 acres; the N.E.1/4 of the S.E.1/2, Section 26, Township 2 North, Range 1 West, containing 40 acres, and all other real property and any right, title or interest therein, of which I may be possessed at the time of my death.

Her
MAGGIE REED [thumb print]
Mark.

We, Fred A. Baker, and Jewell D. Martin, the Post Office Address of both of us being Fort Duchesne, Utah, do hereby certify that Maggie Reed signed the above will in our presence, and declared at that time that this instrument was her last will and testament; that we sign this will at the request of Maggie Reed, in her presence and in the presence of each other.

Witnesses

Jewell D. Martin P.O. Fort Duchesne, Utah.
　　　Supervisor in charge.
Fred A Baker P.O. Fort Duchesne, Utah.
　　　Special Indian Agent.

Department of The Interior,
Office of Indian Affairs, Washington,
FEB 28 1914

The within will is hereby recommended for approval in accordance with the provisions of the Act of June 25, 1910 (36 Stats. L., 855-6) as amended by Act of February 14, 1913 (37 Stats. L., 678).

Respectfully,
EB Meritt
Assistant Commissioner

Department of The Interior
Office of The Secretary MAR -2 1914
The within will is hereby approved in accordance with the provisions of the Act of June 25, 1910 (36 Stats. L., 855-6) as amended by Act of February 14, 1913 (37 Stats. L., 678).

Suirus Saylin
Assistant Secretary

PETER LINDSEY

IN THE NAME OF GOD, AMEN:

I, Peter Lindsey[sic], of Umatilla, Oregon, at the age of 79 years and being of sound and disposing mind and memory, and not acting under stress, menace, fraud or undue influence, of any person whatever, do make, publish and declare this my LAST WILL AND TESTAMENT, in manner following, that is to say:-

First:- I direct that my body be decently buried with proper regard to my station and condition in life, and the circumstances of my estate.

Second:- I direct that my funeral expenses and expenses of my last sickness and all my just debts be paid out of my estate after the property hereinafter named has been taken out.

Third:- I give, devise and bequeath the following:-

Commencing at a point fifteen chains due north of the Southeast corner of Section Thirty Four, Township Thirty Four, North Range Three East thence due west twenty chains of Boise Meridian thence due north ten chains; thence due east twenty chains; thence due south ten chains; to the place of beginning.

TO MY GRAND SON Robert Lindsey[sic], because he has been good and kind to me in my old age and because I may soon depart from this earth.

IN WITNESS WHEREOF, I have hereunto put my hand and seal this 10th day of February, 1917.

Peter Lindsley (Seal)

Witness   *Mc Coy Hill*
           John J Lawyer

99

The foregoing instrument consisting of one sheet of paper was at the date hereof, by the said Peter Lindsey, signed, sealed and published and declared to be his LAST WILL AND TESTAMENT, in the presence of us, and at his request and in his presence and in the presence of each other have subscribed our names thereunto as witnesses on this 10th day of February, 1917.

McCoy Hill
Residing at Kamiah, Idaho
John J Lawyer
Residing at Kamiah, Idaho

Department of The Interior,
Office of Indian Affairs, Washington,
APR 25 1917

The within will of Peter Lindsley, Nez Perce allottee #361, is hereby recommended for approval in accordance with the provisions of the Act of June 25, 1910 (36 Stats. L., 855-6) as amended by Act of February 14, 1913 (37 Stats. L., 678).

Respectfully,
C F Hawke
Assistant Commissioner

Department of The Interior
Office of The Secretary MAY 16 1917

The within will of Peter Lindsley, Nez Perce allottee #361, is hereby approved in accordance with the provisions of the Act of June 25, 1910 (36 Stats. L., 855-6) as amended by Act of February 14, 1913 (37 Stats. L., 678).

Franklin K Payne
Secretary

OFFICE OF INDIAN AFFAIRS
RECEIVED
(Date Illegible)
18964

MRS. RED EYE

LAST WILL AND TESTAMENT OF MRS. RED EYE.

I, Mrs. Red Eye, of Canadian County, State of Oklahoma, being now in fair health, sound in mind and body, do hereby make, publish, and declare this as my last will abd[sic] testament, hereby revoking any other wills by me made.

First: I give, devise and bequeath to my grand-son, Glen Lumpmouth, the following: East half of the South-east quarter of Sec. 27, Twp. 13 North of Range 12, W.I.M., containing 80 acres.

Second: I give and bequeath to my grand-son, Jimmie Lumpmouth, the following: West half of the South-east quarter of Sec. 27, Twp. 13 North of Range 12, W.I.M., containing 80 acres.

Third: I give, devise and bequeath any other property that I may posses[sic] at my death, to my lawful heirs who survive me.

IN WITNESS WHEREOF, I, Mrs. Red Eye, subscribe my name by thumb mark, this eighth day of January 1917.   *her*

Mrs. Red Eye [thumb print]
                                        mark

Subscribed by Mrs. Red Eye the above named in presence of us the undersigned, and in the presence of each other, and at the request of Mrs. Red Eye have subscribed our names as witnesses to the above.

Robert Burns
W.B. Mͨ Coron
David H Todd

Department of The Interior,
Office of Indian Affairs, Washington,
                    APR -7 1920
It is recommended that the within will of Mrs. Red Eye, be approved in accordance with the Act of June 25, 1910 (36 Stats. L., 855-6) as amended by Act of February 14, 1913 (37 Stats. L., 678), and the Regulations of the Department.

Respectfully,
EB Meritt
Assistant Commissioner

Department of The Interior
Office of The Secretary APR 23 1920

The within will of Mrs. Red Eye is hereby approved in accordance with the Act of June 25, 1910 (36 Stats. L., 855-6) as amended by Act of February 14, 1913 (37 Stats. L., 678), and the Regulations of the Department.

SG Hopkins
Assistant Secretary

▲▼▲▼▲▼▲▼▲▼▲▼▲▼

JOSEPH STEVE or JOSEPH STENE

Original

WILL OF JOSEPH STEVE.

Be it remembered that I, Joseph Steve, sometimes known as Joseph Stene, Roseburg allottee No. 98, aged 52 years, and residing at Siletz, Oregon, being of sound mind and acting under no duress or undue influence, do hereby voluntary[sic] declare this to be my last will and testament.

I give, devise and bequeath unto my first cousin, Mary Dick, Siletz Allottee No. 131 (the wife of William Dick) any and all property, real and personal, which I possess, or of which I may be possessed at the time of my death, and described as follows:

(1) My own allotment No. 98, (Roseburg District) containing 160 acres, located in Curry County, Oregon, and valued at approximately $3500.00.

(2) The sum of $500.00, being $100.00 from each of the allotments of John Captain, Sarah Captain, John Skelly, Catherine Skelly and Francis Sutton, bequeathed me by Francis Sutton in her will dated February 5, 1914 and approved February 1, 1917. (Las-Heir. 129037-16)

(3) Any and all property of which I might die possessed.

Witness my hand and seal, this 25th day of June, 1917.

Joseph Steve 🖤

WITNESSES TO SIGNITURE[sic]:
V M Pinkley, Physician
Siletz, Oregon

Robert (Illegible), Teacher
Siletz, Oregon

Signed, sealed, published and declared by Joseph Steve (Joseph Stene) as and for this last will and testament in our presence, and in the presence of each of us, on this 25th day of June, 1917.

V M Pinkley, Physician
Siletz, Oregon
Robert (Illegible), Teacher
Siletz, Oregon
Arthur Bensell
Siletz, Oregon
(Signature Illegible)
Siletz, Oregon

Department of The Interior,
Office of Indian Affairs, Washington,
APR 14 1920
The within will of Joseph Steve, or Joseph Stene, is hereby recommended for approval in accordance with the Act of June 25, 1910 (36 Stats. L., 855-6) as amended by Act of February 14, 1913 (37 Stats. L., 678).

Respectfully,
EB Meritt
Assistant Commissioner

Department of The Interior
Office of The Secretary   APR 15 1920

The within will of Joseph Steve, or Joseph Stene, is hereby approved in accordance with the Act of June 25, 1910 (36 Stats. L., 855-6) as amended by Act of February 14, 1913 (37 Stats. L., 678).

SG Hopkins
Assistant Secretary

▲▼▲▼▲▼▲▼▲▼▲▼▲▼

AGNES STRIKE

LAST WILL OF AGNES STRIKE.

I Agnes Strike, of the State of South Dakota and County of Charles Mix, being of sound mind and memory, do hereby make and declare this to be me[sic] last will and testiment[sic], hereby revoking any and all wills heretofore made by me.

First: I will and bequeath to my niece Mary Frederick the sum $2000.oo [sic] from any money on deposit to my credit with the Superintendent of the Yankton Agency, Greenwood, So. Dak.

Second: I will and bequeath to my Grand niece Mrs Louisa Hope the sum of $3000.oo[sic] to be paid from any funds to my credit with the Superintendent, Yankton Agency.

Third: I will and bequeath to Baptiste Hope the sum of $2000.oo[sic] to be paid from any funds to my credit with the Superintendent Yankton Indian Agency at the time of my death.

Fourth: I direct that all just debts that have be incurred recently be paid, together with my funeral expenses, and that a monument be erected to my grave at a cost of $200.oo and that all moneys remaining be divided equally between Mrs Louisa Hope and Mary Frederick.

Fifth: I will and bequeath my undivided 1/3 interest in the estate of Tobacco Smoke Res Yankton Allottee No. 197 to Mrs. Louisa Hope, Mary Frederick and Baptiste Hope.

Sixth: I will and bequeath the house in which I live together with all furniture and fixtures to Helen Chinn.

IN TESTIMONY WHEREOF I have set my hand and seal this 23rd, day of May 1918.

her

Agnes Strike [thumb print]

mark

Signed Sealed Published and Declared this 23rd day of May 1918 by the said Agnes Strike, in our presence as and for her last will and testament, and at her request and in her presence and in the presence of each other we have subscribed our names as attesting witnesses.

John McBride Sr	Dante, South Dakota.
Emmett E McNeilly	Wagner, South Dakota.

Department of the Interior,
Office of Indian Affairs, Washington, APR 10 1920

It is hereby recommended that the within will of Agnes Strike, deceased Yankton Sioux allottee No. 619, be approved under the provisions of the Act of June 25, 1910 (36 Stats. L. 855-6) as amended by Act of February 14, 1913 (37 Stats. L. 678), and the Regulations of the Department.

> Respectfully,
> *EB Meritt*
> Assistant Commissioner

Department of The Interior
Office of The Secretary, Washington

APR 12 1920

The within will of Agnes Strike, deceased Yankton Sioux allottee No. 619, is hereby approved under the provisions of the Act of June 25, 1910 (36 Stats. L. 855-6) as amended by Act of February 14, 1913 (37 Stats. L. 678), and the Regulations of the Department.

> *SG Hopkins*
> Assistant Secretary

WABAST

OFFICE OF INDIAN AFFAIRS
RECEIVED
OCT 31 1919
93441

Dunseith, N Dak
August 6th, 1914

Last will and testiment[sic] of
Wabast:--

I will all my land to my two children to be divided equally between them. - Nothing to be left to my husband, Victor Loquart - I leave children to mother for.

> her
> *Wabast* [thumb print]
> mark

Witnesses
    Opposite the Day

his
[thumb print]
mark

his

Machifeness   [thumb print]

mark

her

Tapishco   [thumb print]

mark

PROBATE
93441 - 1919
  L L

Department of The Interior,
Office of Indian Affairs, Washington,

MAR 29 1920

It is recommended that the within will be approved pursuant to the provisions of the Act of June 25, 1910 (36 Stats. L., 855-6) as amended by Act of February 14, 1913 (37 Stats. L., 678).

Respectfully,
EB Meritt
Assistant Commissioner

Department of The Interior
Office of The Secretary   APR -9 1920

The within will is approved pursuant to the provisions of the Act of June 25, 1910 (36 Stats. L., 855-6) as amended by Act of February 14, 1913 (37 Stats. L., 678).

SG Hopkins
Assistant Secretary

▲▼▲▼▲▼▲▼▲▼▲▼▲▼

SUNKAMAKOMANI

LAST WILL AND TESTAMENT
OF
SUNKAMAKOMANI, -- ALLOTTEE NO. 1154.

IN THE NAME OF GOD, AMEN.

Indian Wills, 1911 – 1921 Book Six
Records of The Bureau of Indian Affairs

I, Sunkamakomani, of Fort Totten, North Dakota, born 1843, being of sound mind, memory and understanding, do hereby make and publish this my last Will and Testament, hereby revoking and annulling all wills by me heretofore made, in manner and form following, that is to say:

First, I direct that all my just bedts[sic] and funeral expenses and expenses of my last illness shall be paid by my executor hereinafter named as soon after my decease as shall be convenient;

Second, I give devise and bequeath to my Grandson, Alexander Yankton, age 26 years, son of my daughter, Tunkandutawin, deceased, all of my undivided interest in the estate o my deceased Wife, Tawacinhawin, Devils Lake Sioux allottee No. 1155.

Third, I give devise and bequeath Alexander Yankton, grandson, age 26 years, the SW1/4 of SW1/4 Sec. 23, Twp. 153, N., Range 67 W., 5th P.M., North Dakota, being a part of my allotment No. 1154.

Fourth: I give devise and bequeath to Felix Irish, age 13 years, my grandson, the son of my deceased daughter Tunkandutawin, the SE1/4 of SW1/4 Sec. 23, Twp. 153 N., R. 67 W., 5th P.M., North Dakota.

Fifth, I give, devise and bequeath to my wife, Mekwanmekapawit, the NE1/4 of NW1/4 Sec. 26, Twp. 153 N., R. 67 W., 5th P.M., North Dakota, being a part of my allotment No. 1154.

Sixth, I give devise and bequeath to my Great Grandson Andrew Yankton, age 1 year, the son of my grandson, Alexander Yankton, Lot 1 (NW1/4 of NW1/4) Sec. 26, Twp. 153 N., R. 67 W., 5th P.M., North Dakota, being a part of my allotment No. 1154.

And Lastly, I do hereby nominate, constitute and appoint Alexander Yankton executor of this my last Will and Testament.

IN TESTIMONY WHEREOF, I have set my hand and seal to this my last Will and Testament, at Fort Totten, North Dakota, this 5th day of May, in the year of our Lord 1917.   his

Sunkamakomani[thumb print]

mark

Signed, Sealed, Published and Declared by the said Sunkamakomani in our presence, as and for his last Will and Testament, and at his request and in our presence, and in the presence of each other, we have hereunto subscribed our names as attesting witnesses thereto.

Sam Young   *Catharine (Illegible)*
                                    Charles Picard

Department of The Interior,
Office of Indian Affairs, Washington,
                    AUG 31 1916
It is recommended that the within will be approved pursuant to the provisions of the Act of June 25, 1910 (36 Stats. L., 855-6) as amended by Act of February 14, 1913 (37 Stats. L., 678).

                              Respectfully,
                              EB Meritt
                              Assistant Commissioner
Department of The Interior AUG 31 1916
Office of The Secretary

The within will is hereby approved pursuant to the provisions of the Act of June 25, 1910 (36 Stats. L., 855-6) as amended by Act of February 14, 1913 (37 Stats. L., 678).

                              SG Hopkins
                              Assistant Secretary

JUAN PERMAMSU

OFFICE OF INDIAN AFFAIRS
RECEIVED
MAR 28 1918
26775

LAST   WILL   AND   TESTAMENT

Lawton, Okla.

I, Juan Permansu[sic], of Lawton, Comanche County, Oklahoma, about 24 years of age, now in good health, strength of body and mind, but sensible of the uncertainty of life and desiring to make disposition of my property and affairs while in health and strength, do hereby make, publish and declare the following to be my last will and testament, hereby revoking and cancelling all other or former wills by me at any time made.

1.   I direct the payment of all my just debts and funeral expenses.

2.   I give and devise to my beloved father, Per-mam-su (Comanche Jack) Comanche allottee No. 2025, 1/2 of all of my property, real and personal, of which I may die possessed and direct that the E/2 of my allotment, comprising the SW/4-21-1S-13, go to my said father as his share of my estate after my death.

3.   I give and devise to my belovee[sic] mother, Pe-pe, Comanche allottee 2026, 1/2 of all my property of which I may die possessed, real and personal, and direct that the W/2 of my said allotment, referred to in the foregoing devise, go to my said mother as her share of said allotment.

This will is made subject to the approval of the Secretary of the Interior.

In witness whereof, I, Juan Per-mam-su, have to this my last will and testament, consisting of two (2) sheets of paper, subscribed my name this *21* day of *March*, 1918.   *his*

Juan Permamsu [thumb print]
mark

Subscribed by Juan Permamsu in the presence of each of us the undersigned and at the same time declared by him to us to be his last will and testament, and we thereupon at the request of Juan Permamsu, in his presence and in the presence of each other, sign our names hereto as witnesses this *21* day of *March*, 1918, at Lawton, Comanche County, Oklahoma.

Earl Nease
P.O. *Lawton, Okla.*
Antonio Martinez
P.O. *Lawton, Okla.*

Department of The Interior,
Office of Indian Affairs, Washington,
APR 10 1920

It is recommended that the within will be approved pursuant to the provisions of the Act of June 25, 1910 (36 Stats. L., 855-6) as amended by Act of February 14, 1913 (37 Stats. L., 678), and the Regulations of the Department.

Respectfully,

EB Meritt

Assistant Commissioner

Department of The Interior

Office of The Secretary APR 13 1920

The within will is approved pursuant to the provisions of the Act of June 25, 1910 (36 Stats. L., 855-6) as amended by Act of February 14, 1913 (37 Stats. L., 678), and the Regulations of the Department.

SG Hopkins

Assistant Secretary

▲▼▲▼▲▼▲▼▲▼▲▼▲▼▲▼

LUCY PRUNER

LAST WILL AND TESTAMENT OF LUCY J. PRUNER.

I, Lucy J. Pruner of Anadarko, in the County of Caddo, State of Oklahoma, being now in good health, strength of body and mind, but sensible of the uncertainty of life, and desiring to make disposition of my property and affairs while in health and strength, do hereby make, publish and declare this my last will and testament, hereby revoking and cancelling all other and former wills by me at any time made.

(First.) I direct the payment of all my just debts and funeral expenses.

(Second.) I give and bequeath to my beloved husband H.P. Pruner, the $3000.00 on deposit with the Government which I inherited from the sale of my deceased sister's lands.

(Third.) All the residue of my estate, real, personal, and mixed I give and bequeath unto my four children John R. Osborn, Margaret McLane, Mattie Sturm, and Chas. B. Pruner and my two foster children, Frank Osborn and Emma Osborn to share in the following proportion; and in case of the death of any of my said children, the share shall be divided among the children of such child; but in case of the death of either of my said foster children, then such legacy shall lapse; To John R. Osborn, Margaret McLane, Mattie Sturm and Chas. B. Pruner, each one fifth, and to Frank Osborn and Emma Osborn, each one tenth.

(Fourth.) I authorize my executors hereinafter named, to sell and dispose of all of my land for the purpose of making distribution as herein ordered.

(Fifth.) I hereby appoint and designate my two sons John R. Osborn and Chas B. Pruner, joint executors of this my last will and testament and direct that they be not required to give **any** bond.

In Witness whereof, I, Lucy J. Pruner have to this my last will and testament consisting of two pages subscribed my name this 6th day of February, 1918.

her
Lucy J. X Pruner
mark

Witness to signature written by me
C. Ross Hume,
Witness G.E. Porter

Department of The Interior,
Office of Indian Affairs, Washington,

APR 3- 1920

It is hereby recommended that the within will of Lucy J. Pruner, deceased allottee No. 65 of the Wichita Tribe, be approved under the provisions of the Act of June 25, 1910 (36 Stats. L., 855-6) as amended by Act of February 14, 1913 (37 Stats. L., 678), and the Regulations of the Department.

Respectfully,
EB Meritt
Assistant Commissioner

Department of The Interior
Office of The Secretary APR 13 1920

The within will of Lucy J. Pruner, deceased allottee No. 65 of the Wichita Tribe, is hereby approved under the provisions of the Act of June 25, 1910 (36 Stats. L., 855-6) as amended by Act of February 14, 1913 (37 Stats. L., 678), and the Regulations of the Department.

SG Hopkins
Assistant Secretary

▲▼▲▼▲▼▲▼▲▼▲▼▲▼

HAU-ZIP-PAH

Indian Wills, 1911 – 1921 Book Six
Records of The Bureau of Indian Affairs

LAST WILL AND TESTAMENT.

- - - oOo - - -

Anadarko, Okla., May 30, 1918.

I, Hau-zip-pah, Kiowa Indian allottee No. 2169, of Kiowa County, being now in good health, strength of body and mind, but sensible of the uncertainty of life and desiring to make disposition of my property and affairs while in health and strength, do hereby make, publish, and declare the following to be my last will and testament, hereby revoking and cancelling all other or former wills by me at any time made.

First; I direct the payment of all my just debts and funeral expenses.

Second: I give and devise all of my rights, title, and interest in and to the SE/4 of Section 34, Township 4 North, of Range 13, being Kiowa allottment No. 2168, to my beloved daughter, Fannie Tah-po-mah, Kiowa Indian allottee No. 1241. This land was originally allotted to Pah-ko-to-quodle, who was my husband. After his death the Department in L.H. 8067-14 E. G. T. declared that I was entitled to one-half (1/2) of said estate.

Third: I give and devise in equal shares to my grandson, Weiser Tong-ke-am-ha, Family No. 21, Kiowa, and to my beloved husband, Mo-be-adle-ky, Kiowa Indian allottee No. 1816, all of my rights, title, and interest in and to the SW/4 of Section 25, Township 4 North, of Range 13. This is my trust allotment of land, known upon the rolls of the Interior Department as Kiowa Indian allotment No. 2169. My reason for devising a part interest in and to said allotment to my grandson is that said grandson has received no allotment of land on the Kiowa Indian reservation or any other Indian reservation in the United States. I desire that he receive the benefit of a part of an allotment and have therefore decided to devise a part of my allotment to him. These devises have been made after mature deliberation and after consulting my husband and my daughter fully and freely in the matter.

I give and bequeath all the residue and remainder of my property of which I may die possessed in equal shares to the above names beneficiaries, to wit: (a) To my husband, Mo-be-adle-ky, Kiowa Indian allottee No. 1816, one-third (1/3); (b) To my daughter, Fannie Tah-po-mah, Kiowa Indian allottee No. 1241, one-third (1/3); To my grandson, Weiser Tong-ke-am-ha, an unallotted Kiowa Indian, one-third (1/3).

This will is made subject to the approval of the Seretary[sic] of the Interior.

In witness whereof, I, Hau-zip-pah, have to this, my last will and testament, consisting of three sheets of paper subscribe[sic] my name this 30th day of May, 1918, at Kiowa Indian Agency, Anadarko, Okla.

her

Hau-zip-pah [thumb print]

mark.

WITNESSES:

H.E. Bretschneider   *Parker MᶜKenzie*

Subscribed by Hau-zip-pah, in the presence of each of us, the undersigned, and at the same time declared by her to us to be her last will and testament, and we thereupon at the request of Hau-zip-pah in her presence and in the presence of each other sign our names hereto as witnesses this 30th day of May, 1918, at the Kiowa Indian Agency, Anadarko, Oklahoma.

H.E. Bretschneider

P.O. Kiowa Agency, Anadarko, Oklahoma

Parker MᶜKenzie

P.O. Kiowa Agency, Anadarko, Oklahoma

INTERPRETOR'S[sic] CERTIFICATE.

I, *Parker MᶜKenzie*, hereby certify on honor that I acted as interpretor[sic] during the execution of the foregoing last will and testament by Hau-zip-pah; that I interpreted fully and correctly all the contents of said will before it was executed by her, and that the devises therein contained were written in said will strictly in accordance with her desires and directions. I further certify that I speak both the Kiowa Indian as well as the English languages fluently.

Signed this 30th day of May, 1918.

Parker MᶜKenzie

Interpretor[sic].

Department of The Interior,
Office of Indian Affairs, Washington,

APR 22 1920

It is recommended that the within will of Hau-zip-pah, be approved with the Act of June 25, 1910 (36 Stats. L., 855-6) as amended by Act of February 14, 1913 (37 Stats. L., 678), and the Regulations of the Department.

Respectfully,
EB Meritt
Assistant Commissioner

Department of The Interior
Office of The Secretary   APR 22 1920

The within will of Hau-zip-pah, is hereby approved in accordance with the Acts of June 25, 1910 (36 Stats. L., 855-6) as amended by Act of February 14, 1913 (37 Stats. L., 678), and the Regulations of the Department.

SG Hopkins
Assistant Secretary

▲▼▲▼▲▼▲▼▲▼▲▼▲▼▲▼

MARY FEATHER EAR RING TWO BULLS

W I L L.

IN THE NAME OF GOD, AMEN:

I, Mary Two Bulls, Fort Peck allottee No. 335, being of sound mind but infirm of body and realizing the uncertainty of life, and not acting under fraud, menace, duress, or undue influence, do this 11th day of April, 1916, in the presence of the witnesses who have attached their names to this instrument, make, declare and publish this my last will and testament, that is to say:

First: I give, devise and bequeath my timber and grazing allotments to my husband, Charles Two Bulls, Fort Peck allottee No. 1884, and to my son John Two Bulls, Fort Peck allottee No. 2219, in equal shares, share and share alike, said timber land described as Lot 8, Sec. 2, T. 27 N, R. 49 E., containing 22.55 acres; said grazing allotment being described as the S/2 of Sec. 13, T. 29 N., R. 47 E., containing 320 acres.

Second: I give, devise, and bequeath unto my father and mother, Feather ear ring and Red seat Feather earring, Fort Peck allottees Nos. 331 and 332, in equal shares, share and share alike, my irrigable allotment

114

described as the NW/4 of the SE/4 of Sec. 5, T. 27 N., R. 49 E, containing 40 acres. My reason for devising a part of my land to my father and mother is that they have taken care of me and provided for me during the past few months when I have been and when my husband was unable to give me the care and support that I needed.

Third: All other property or interest in property of which I may die possessed, I give, devise and bequeath unto my husband, Charles Two Bulls and my son John Two Bulls, in equal shares, share and share alike.

Witness my hand and seal this 11th day of April, 1916.

Her

Witness to signature:	*Mary Two Bulls* [thumb print]
Burton F. Roth	Fort Peck allottee No. 335.*Thumb*
Poplar, Montana.	
Claude M Reddoor , Interpreter.	
Poplar, Montana.	

We, the undersigned, depose and say that we are in no way related to the testatrix, Mary Two Bulls, and that we were present and witnessed the signing of the above will in one page, that the same was fully interpretted[sic] to and read to and by the testatrix, and that she fully understood the same, that we believe the testatrix was acting of her own free will and accord, and not under undue influence whatsoever, that the within instrument was signed in our presence and in the presence of one another this 11th day of April, 1916.

Burton F. Roth
Claude M Reddoor

Department of The Interior,
Office of Indian Affairs, Washington,
APR 29 1920

The within will of Mary Feather Ear Ring Two Bulls, deceased Fort Peck Yankton Sioux allottee No. 335, of the Fort Peck Reservation, is recommended for approval in accordance with the provisions of the Act of June 25, 1910 (36 Stats. L., 855-6) as amended by Act of February 14, 1913 (37 Stats. L., 678).

Respectfully,
EB Meritt
Assistant Commissioner

Department of The Interior
Office of The Secretary APR 30 1920

The within will of Mary Feather Ear Ring Two Bulls, deceased Fort Peck Yankton Sioux allottee No. 335, of the Fort Peck Reservation, is hereby approved in accordance with the provisions of the Act of June 25, 1910 (36 Stats. L., 855-6) as amended by Act of February 14, 1913 (37 Stats. L., 678).

*SG Hopki*ns
Assistant Secretary

▲▼▲▼▲▼▲▼▲▼▲▼▲

OFFICE OF INDIAN AFFAIRS
RECEIVED
MAY 6- 1920
39060

REDLIGHTNING or JACOB REDLIGHTNING

I, Redlightning **or Jacob Redlightning,** of Charles Mix County, State of south Dakota, being of sound mind and memory, do make, publish, and declare this to be my last will and testament, hereby revoking all previous will[sic] made by me.

First: I give and bequeath to my Grand-daughter, Phoebe Redlightning, the following described real estate in Charles Mix County, State of South Dakota, to wit: Lots numbered Two and Three, (2 and 3) in Section Thirty-two (32), Township Ninety-five, (95), North of Range Sixty-four, (64), containing 48.56 acres, being the allotment of my deceased son, Edward Redlightning; Also Lot number Two Hundred Ninety-five (295) or the North east quarter of the North west quarter, (NE/4 of NW/4) of Section Thirty-two, Township Ninety-five, North of Range Sixty-four, this being a portion of my own allotment containing 40 acres, making a total of 88.56 acres.

Second: I give and bequeath to my Grand-son, Martin Redlightning, the following described real estate in Charles Mix County, State of South Dakota, to-wit: North east quarter of the South east quarter *in Section 6*; Lots numbered Three and Four of Section Five, and the Lot numbered Three Hundred Sixteen or the South east quarter of the North east quarter, and the South east quarter of the South east quarter, all in Section Six, Township Ninety-four, North of Range Sixty-four, containing in all 123.76 acres.

Third: I give and bequeath to my Grand-daughter, Lorena M. Redlightning, the following described real estate in Charles Mix County, State of South Dakota, to-wit: South east quarter of the North east quarter of Section Twelve, Township Ninety-four, North of Range Sixty-five, which was allotted to my deceased wife, Tewastewin, and the North east quarter of the North east quarter of Section Seven, Township Ninety-four, North of Range Sixty-four of my own allotment, containing in all 80 acres.

Fourth: I give, devise and bequeath unto my legal heirs all the residue of my property, both real and personal, after my death and burial, requesting that all my just debts and funeral expenses are paid by my executor herein after named.

Fifth: I hereby appoint, G.W. Williamson, of Greenwood, South Dakota, as executor, empowering him to act as much.

IN TESTIMONY WHEREOF, I HEREUNTO SET my hand and seal, and publish and declare this to be my last will and testament, revoking all other wills made by me, in the presence of the witnesses named below this 14th day of FEBRUARY 1914.   his [thumb print]
Interpreter: REDLIGHTNING OR JACOB REDLIGHTNING
Thomas Redlightning   mark

Signed, Sealed and Declared by the said Jacob Redlightning as and for his last Will and Testament in presence of us, who at his request and in his presence and in the presence of each other, have subscribed our names as witnesses hereto:

WB McCown   , Greenwood, South Dakota.
Charlotte Schulz , Greenwood, South Dakota.

Department of The Interior,
Office of Indian Affairs, Washington,
                    JUN 3 1914
It is recommended that the within will be approved pursuant to the provisions of the Act of June 25, 1910 (36 Stats. L., 855-6) as amended by Act of February 14, 1913 (37 Stats. L., 678).

Respectfully,
EB Meritt
Assistant Commissioner

Department of The Interior
Office of The Secretary

JUN -4 1914

The within will is hereby approved pursuant to the provisions of the Act of June 25, 1910 (36 Stats. L., 855-6) as amended by Act of February 14, 1913 (37 Stats. L., 678).

Suirus Saylin
Assistant Secretary

▲▼▲▼▲▼▲▼▲▼▲▼▲▼

REBECCA KING OR OGLALA

Original
WILL

I, **Rebecca King or Oglala** of Pine Ridge Agency, South Dakota, Allottee number **2846** do hereby make and declare this to be my last will and testament, in accordance with Section 2 of the Act of June 25, 1910, (36 stat. 855-858) and Act of February 14, 1913, (Public No. 381), hereby revoking all former wills made by me:

1. I hereby direct that as soon as possible after my decease, that all my debts, funeral and testamentary expenses be paid out of my personal estate.

2. I give and devise my allotment on the Pine Ridge Reservation, South Dakota, described as follows:

The North half of Section thirty-two in Township thirty-nine North of Range forty-four West of the Sixth Principal Meridian South Dakota, containing three hundred twenty acres. And 1/3 of the heirs of my husband King, No. 956.
in the following manner:

Chas. King	Son	NE	80 acres	
Jefferson King	"	SE	80 "	1/3 of the
Stephen H. King	"	SW	80 "	heirs, No.
Rosa Black Bird	Dau	NW	80 "	956.

3. I give and bequeath all of my personal property of whatsoever nature and wheresoever situated unto ~~My children~~.

4. All the rest of my property, real or personal, now possessed or hereafter acquired, of whatsoever nature and wheresoever situated, I hereby give, devise and bequeath unto *My children as follows:*

Chas King	*One Cow & bay mare*
Jefferson King	*One cow & one gelding & wagon & well or wind*
Stephen H King	*One cow & white mare* *mill*
Rosa Black Bird	*One cow & one gelding & Buggy*

In witness whereof I have hereunto set my hand this *21* day of *February* 1917

(Mark)   *X* [thumb print]
Rebecca King or Oglala

The above statement was, this *21* day of *February* 1917 signed and published by *Rebecca King or Oglala* as *her* last will and testament, in the joint presence of the undersigned, the said *Rebecca King or Oglala* then being of sound and vigorous mind and free from any constraint or compulsion; whereupon we, being without any interest in the matter other than friendship, and being well acquainted with *her* but not members of *her* family, immediately subscribed our names hereto in the presence of each other and of the said testator, for the purpose of attesting the said will, as *she* requested us to do. And that I, *Rebecca King or Oglala* at the testa*tor*'s request, have written *my* name in ink, and that *I* affixed *my* thumb-marks.

Post Office Address

Jonas Holy Rock   **Manderson So Dak.**
William Fire Thunder   **Manderson, So Dak.**

Pine Ridge, South Dakota.
Dec 10 - 1918
I hereby certify that I have fully inquired into the mental competency of the Indian signing the above will; the circumstances attending the execution of the will; the influence that may have induced its execution, and the names of those entitled to share in the estate under the law of descent in South Dakota: reasons for the disposition of the

property proposed by the will differing from disposition had the property descended by operation of law.

I respectfully forward this will with the recommendation that it be …..approved.

> *Henry M. Tidwell*
> Supt. & Spl. Disb. Agent.

Department of The Interior,
Office of Indian Affairs, Washington,
OCT 8 1919

The within will of Rebecca King or Oglala, is hereby recommended for approval in accordance with the provisions of the Act of June 25, 1910 (36 Stats. L., 855-6) as amended by Act of February 14, 1913 (37 Stats. L., 678).

> Respectfully,
> *EB Meritt*
> Assistant Commissioner

Department of The Interior
Office of The Secretary OCT 8 1919

The within will is hereby approved in accordance with the Act of June 25, 1910 (36 Stats. L., 855-6) as amended by Act of February 14, 1913 (37 Stats. L., 678).

> *SG Hopkins*
> Assistant Secretary

▲▼▲▼▲▼▲▼▲▼▲▼▲▼

LIZZIE LUCAS LOVEJOY

DEPARTMENT OF THE INTERIOR

UNITED STATES INDIAN SERVICE

LAST WILL AND TESTAMENT OF
Lizzie Lucas Lovejoy.

IN THE NAME OF GOD, AMEN: I, Lizzie Lucas Lovejoy, of Santee, in the County of Knox, State of Nebraska, considering the uncertainty of this mortal life, and being of sound mind and memory, blessed be God for the same, do make and publish this my last will and testament, in the manner and form following, this is to say:

FIRST: I direct that my funeral charges, the expenses of administering my estate and all my debts be paid out of my personal property. If that be insufficient I authorize my executors, hereinafter named, to sell so much of my real estate as may be necessary for that purpose.

SECOND: I give and bequeath to Mr. C. H. Moody, merchant at Santee, Nebraska, who has furnished me and my small children with provisions and clothing during my sickness, the sum of $300. To my beloved husband, Thomas Lovejoy, and my children, Florence, David, Albert and Ruth, the balance of my property, the same to be divided equally.

THIRD: I hereby appoint my friend, Supt. A. W. Leech, executor of this my last will and testament, hereby revoking all former wills by me made.

IN WITNESS WHEREOF: I have hereunto subscribed my name this 19th day of November in the year of our Lord one thousand nine hundred eighteen.

Lizzie Lucas Lovejoy

We, the undersigned, do hereby certify that Lizzie Lucas Lovejoy, the testatrix, subscribed her name to this instrument in our presence and in the presence of us, and declared at the same time in our presence and hearing that this instrument was her last will and testament, and we at her request sign our names hereto in her presence as attesting witnesses.

William Holmes

Both or Santee,
Nebraska.   *Capt. B. J Young*

Department of The Interior,
Office of Indian Affairs, Washington,
JUN 25 1920

It is hereby recommended that the within will of Lizzie Lucas Lovejoy, deceased Santee Sioux allottee No. 292, be approved according to the provisions of the Act of June 25, 1910 (36 Stats. L., 855-6) as amended by Act of February 14, 1913 (37 Stats. L., 678), and the Regulations of the Department.

Respectfully,

EB Meritt

Assistant Commissioner

Department of The Interior

Office of The Secretary   JUN 30 1920

The within will of Lizzie Lucas Lovejoy, deceased Santee Sioux allottee No. 292, is hereby approved according to the provisions of the Act of June 25, 1910 (36 Stats. L., 855-6) as amended by Act of February 14, 1913 (37 Stats. L., 678), and the Regulations of the Department.

SG Hopkins

Assistant Secretary

▲▼▲▼▲▼▲▼▲▼▲▼▲▼▲▼

SHOOTS ENEMY

LAST WILL AND TESTAMENT OF SHOOTS ENEMY, ALLOTTEE NO. 98.

CROW CREEK SIOUX INDIAN.

SOUTH DAKOTA.

IN THE NAME OF GOD, AMEN:

I, Shoots Enemy, sixty-six years of age, an Indian of the Crow Creek Indian Reservation, in South Dakota, being of sound mind, memory, and understanding, do hereby make and publish this my last Will and Testament, hereby revoking and annuling[sic] all Wills by me heretofore made, in manner and form following, that is to say:

FIRST: I direct that all my just debts and funeral expenses, and expenses of my last illness shall be paid as soon after my decease as shall be convenient.

SECOND: I give, devise and bequeath all my right title and interest in my allotment, described as the North half (N 1/2) of Section five (5), Township One hundred seven (107) North, of Range Seventy-one (71) West of the 5th P.M., South Dakota, to my wife Yellow Hair and to my son Russell Harrison, to be shared equally by them.

THIRD: I give, devise and bequeath all my right title and interest in the allotment of my deceased daughter, Rebecca Shoots Enemy, described as the North-west quarter (NW1/4) of Section Four (4), Township One hundred seven (107) North, of Range Seventy-one (71) West of the 5th P.M., South Dakota, to my son Russell Harrison.

FOURTH: Provided that my interest in the estate of my mother, Miniataojanjanwin, on the Standing Rock Reservation, described as the North-east quarter (NE1/4), of Section Thirty-six (36), in Township Twenty-two (22) North, or Range Twenty-six (26) Easst[sic], is not sold during my life time, I give, devise and bequeath all my right, title and interest therein, to my wife Yellow Hair and to my son Russell Harrison, to be shared equaly[sic] by them.

FIFTH: I give, devise and bequeath all my right title and interest in the estate of my deceased daughter, Wanyaginapapiwin, on the Sisseton reservation, described as the North-west quarter (NW1/4) of Section eight (8), Township One hundred twenty-three (123) North, of Range Fifty-three (53) West of the 5th P.M., South Dakota, to my wife Yellow Hair and to my son Russell Harrison, to be shared equally by them.

AND LASTLY: I am satisfied that the officers of the Department of the Interior of the United States will make proper provisions for the carrying into effect of this my last Will and Testament, and therefore, I have not appointed an executor to administer my estate.

IN TESTIMONY WHEREOF, I have set my hand and seal to this my last Will and Testament at the Crow Creek Agency office at Fort Thompson, S.Dak., this 15th day of June, 1917.　　　　　　　　　His

　　　　　　　　　　　　　　　Shoots Enemy [thumb print]
Witnesses to mark:　　　　　　　　　　　　Mark
　　　P.W. Lightfoot, Clerk
　　　B.H. Dooley, Chief Clerk
Both of Ft. Thompson, S.D.
　　　Signed, sealed, published and declared by the said Shoots Enemy, in our presence, as and for his last Will and Testament, and at his request and in his presence and in the presence of each other we have hereto subscribed our names as attesting witnesses thereto.

　　　　　　　　　　　　　　William Carpenter
　　　　　　　　　　　　　　Ft. Thompson, S. Dak.

Louis Fire
Ft. Thompson, S. Dak.
Peter W. Lightfoot
Ft. Thompson, S. Dak.

PROBATE
17067-1920
    L L

Department of The Interior,
Office of Indian Affairs, Washington,
                          JUN 16 1920
It is recommended that the within will be approved pursuant to the provisions of the Act of June 25, 1910 (36 Stats. L., 855-6) as amended by Act of February 14, 1913 (37 Stats. L., 678).

Respectfully,
EB Meritt
Assistant Commissioner

Department of The Interior
Office of The Secretary
                          JUN 30 1920
The within will is hereby approved pursuant to the provisions of the Act of June 25, 1910 (36 Stats. L., 855-6) as amended by Act of February 14, 1913 (37 Stats. L., 678).

SG Hopkins
Assistant Secretary

▲▼▲▼▲▼▲▼▲▼▲▼▲▼

WOLF TAIL

OFFICE OF INDIAN AFFAIRS
RECEIVED
JUN 28 1919
64635

In, the name of God, Amen. I, Wolf Tail, of the city of Browning, County of Teton, State of Montana, of the age of sixty seven (67) years, and being of sound and disposing mind and memory, and not acting under duress, menace, fraud, or undue influence of any person whatever, do make publish, and declare this my last will and testament in manner following, that is to say:

First: I direct that my executors, as soon as they have sufficient funds in their hands, pay my funeral expenses.

Second: I give my son John, one set of harness, one spring wagon, one farm wagon, one sulky plow, one harrow, one gray mule, livery barn on Lot 3, Block 10, in Browning, Montana, and small house across street north of barn.

Third: I give my son Joe, one Ford Automobile.

Fourth: I give my brother Jim White Calf, four horses.

Fifth: I give my brother John Two Guns, four horses.

Sixth: I give to Chewing Black Bones, two horses.

Seventh: I give to my wife, Katie Pearl Woman, and my sons, Joe and John, and my daughters, Julia and Agnes, the remainder of the horses, equally divided between them, share and share alike.

Eighth: I give to my son Joe, and daughter Agnes, seven cows to be divided equally between them share and share alike.

Ninth: I give to my wife, Katie Pearl Woman, my sons Joe and John, and my daughter Agnes, my allotment of 320 acres of land to be divided equally between them, share and share alike.

Tenth: I give to my wife, Katie Pearl Woman, two sets of harness, one spring wagon, one farm wagon, large house in Browning, Montana, two buckskin mules, all furniture and all the rest, residue and remainder of any real estate or personal property of every name and nature what so ever, owned by me at the time of my death.

I hereby nominate and appoint Charles Simon, and George S. Martin, or Browning, Teton County, the executors of this, my last Will and Testament, and hereby revoke all former wills by me made.

In witness whereof, I have hereunto set my hand and seal, this First day of October, in the year of our Lord, One Thousand Nine Hundred and Eighteen.

his

Wolf Tail [thumb print] <u>Seal</u>

mark

<u>Witness</u> *H.G. Ewing*

<u>Address</u> *Browning, Mont*

<u>Witness</u>   *JP Croff*
<u>Address</u>   *Browning Mont.*

Department of The Interior,
Office of Indian Affairs, Washington,
                    JUN 1- 1920

It is recommended that the within will of Wolf Tail, deceased allottee No. 724 of the Piegan Tribe of Indians, in the State of Montana, be approved in accordance with the provisions of the Act of June 25, 1910 (36 Stats. L., 855-6) as amended by Act of February 14, 1913 (37 Stats. L., 678), and the Regulations of the Department.

> Respectfully,
> *EB Meritt*
> Assistant Commissioner

Department of The Interior
Office of The Secretary   JUN 29 1920

The within will of Wolf Tail, deceased allottee No. 724 of the Piegan Tribe of Indians, in the State of Montana, is hereby approved in accordance with the provisions of the Act of June 25, 1910 (36 Stats. L., 855-6) as amended by Act of February 14, 1913 (37 Stats. L., 678), and the Regulations of the Department.

> *SG Hopkins*
> Assistant Secretary

▲ ▼ ▲ ▼ ▲ ▼ ▲ ▼ ▲ ▼ ▲ ▼ ▲ ▼ ▲ ▼

YOUNG CRANE

LAST WILL AND TESTAMENT

of

Young Crane

IN THE NAME OF GOD, AMEN.

I, *Young Crane* of *Lodge Grass Mont* being of sound mind, memory, and understanding, do hereby make and publish this, my last will and testament, hereby revoking and annulling all wills by me heretofore made, in manner and form following, that is to say:

Indian Wills, 1911 – 1921 Book Six
Records of The Bureau of Indian Affairs

First; I direct that all of my just debts and funeral expenses, and expenses of my last illness shall be paid by my executor, as soon after my decease as convenient.

Second; I give, devise and bequeath to: *My granddaughter Polly Grasshopper the following described lands: N1/2 of SW1/4 Sec 14, Twp 6S, R. 35 E allot no. 1373 being 80 acres.*

(Third) All personal property of which I may die possesst[sic] I bequeath to my granddaughter Polly Grasshopper above mentioned. Fourth All the residue of my real estate of whatsoever kind or nature I bequeath to my son Packs The Hat.

Third; All the rest and residue of my estate, both real, and personal and mixed, I give devise and bequeath to my lawful heirs as determined after my decease.

And lastly: I do hereby nominate, constitute and appoint *Evan W Estep, Supt or his successor in office* executor of this my last will and testament.

In testimony whereof, I have set my hand and seal to this, my last will and Testament, at *Lodge Grass* Montana, this *22nd* day of *Nov* in the year of our Lord one thousand nine hundred and *Sixteen*.

His
Young Crane [thumb print]
Mark

Signed, sealed, published and declared by said *Young Crane* in our presence, as and for *his* last Will and testament, and at *his* request and in our presence, and in the presence of each other, we have hereunto subscribed our names as attesting witnesses thereto.

SPCope Farmer	of	*Lodge Grass*
George Hill	of	*Lodge Grass*
Anna A. Cope	of	*Lodge Grass*

Department of The Interior,
Office of Indian Affairs, Washington,

JUN 25 1920

It is hereby recommended that the within will of Young Crane, deceased Crow allottee No. 1373, be approved under the provisions of the Act of

June 25, 1910 (36 Stats. L., 855-6) as amended by Act of February 14, 1913 (37 Stats. L., 678), and the Regulations of the Department.

Respectfully,
EB Meritt
Assistant Commissioner

Department of The Interior
Office of The Secretary

The within will of Young Crane, deceased Crow allottee No. 1373, is approved under the provisions of the Act of June 25, 1910 (36 Stats. L., 855-6) as amended by Act of February 14, 1913 (37 Stats. L., 678), and the Regulations of the Department.

SG Hopkins
Assistant Secretary

▲▼▲▼▲▼▲▼▲▼▲▼▲▼▲▼

JOHN BUCKSKIN or N-PUK-A-PUK-A-CHIN

Will.
Spokane,
John Buckskin.

I, John Buckskin, or N-puk-a-puk-a-chin, being of sound and disposing mind and memory, do hereby will, devise and bequeath to my grandson, John Alexander, all of my Spokane Allotment No. 161, described as follows:

The northeast quarter of the southeast quarter (NE1/4 - SE1/4) of Section Six (6), the southwest quarter of the northeast quarter of the southwest quarter (SW1/4-NE1/4-SW1/4); the southeast quarter of the northwest quarter of the southwest quarter (SE1/4-NW1/4-SW1/4) and the northwest quarter of the southeast quarter of the southwest quarter (NW1/4-SE1/4-SW1/4) of Section Nine (9); all in Township Twenty-seven (27) North, Range Thirty-nine (39) E.W.M., containing eighty (80) acres.

Colville Agency, Washington.　　　　　　　　　　　　　*his right*
　　May 5, 1911.　　　　　　　　　　　　　　　　[thumb print]
　　　　　　　　　　　　　　　　　John Buckskin　thumb mark
WITNESSES:　　　　　　　　　　　　　　*N-puk-a-puk-a-chin*
　　Lester B. Vincent

Dan Sherwood

Department of the Interior,
Office of Indian Affairs, Washington,

JUL 22 1911

I hereby recommend that the within will be approved under the provisions of Section 2 of the Act of June 25, 1910, 36 Stat. L., 855-858.

Respectfully,
CF Hawke
Acting Commissioner

Approved   JUL 29 1911

Samuel Adams
First Assistant Secretary

Department of The Interior
Office of The Secretary, Washington   JUN 30 1920

Department approval, dated July 22, 1911, of the within will of John Buckskin, is hereby withdrawn for the reason that the beneficiary, John Alexander, died before testator, and the said will is hereby disapproved, according to the Act of June 25, 1910 (36 Stat. L., 855).

SG Hopkins
Assistant Secretary

▲▼▲▼▲▼▲▼▲▼▲▼▲▼

CHOTOWIZI

W I L L.

IN THE NAME OF GOD AMEN:

I, **Chotowizi**, Fort Peck allottee No. **242** residing at **Poplar, Mont.** Montana, being of sound mind but of feeble health and realizing the uncertainty of life, and not acting under fraud, duress, menace or undue influence, do this **6** of **May**, 1918, make, publish and declare the following to be my last will and testament:

Indian Wills, 1911 – 1921 Book Six
Records of The Bureau of Indian Affairs

First:

I give, devise and bequeath

To my wife Mrs. Chotowizi the forth acres described as follows NW of SE Sec 11, 27-50 and upon whih[sic] my home now stands. Also the twenty acres of my timber allotment described as follows E1/2 NE of NW of Sec. 14-27-50

also to my wife all persoal[sic] property in my possession and moneys in my credit at the time of my death.

Second:

I give, devise and bequeath

to my wife Mrs. Chotowizi, my daughter-in-law, Mrs. Andrew Red Bull, and her youngest present living child, Joseph Red Bull, share and share alike, My grazing Allotment described as follows W 1/2 of Sec. 25-32-49

and my share in the allotments of my children described as follows Sec. 35-29-50

and the NW of SW of 17-27-59 and SE of NE 10-27-50 to Joseph Redbull the forty acres described as follows

and lastly I devise and bequeath to my wife all property inherited or otherwie[sic] not otherwise provided for in this will to which I am now or may be declared the heir.

I hereby appoint E.D. Mossman, Supt. of Fort Peck Agency, or his successor in office, as executor of my estate. *mark*

Chotowizi his]thumb print]

Fort Peck Allottee No........

Witness:

Peter Dupree

Patrick Hamley

We, the undersigned, hereby certify on our honor that neither of us are related in any way to the testator that we were both present and witnessed the signature of the testator to the above instrument in one page which **he** read and fully understood before signing as **he** was apparently of sound mind and signed the same of **his** own free will and accord stating that **his** wishes were duly set forth.

Peter Dupree
Patrick Hamley

Department of The Interior,
Office of Indian Affairs, Washington,
JUN 21 1920

The within will of Chotowizi, deceased Yankton Sioux allottee No. 242, of the Fort Peck Reservation, is recommended for approval in accordance with the provisions of the Act of June 25, 1910 (36 Stats. L., 855-6) as amended by Act of February 14, 1913 (37 Stats. L., 678).

Respectfully,
EB Meritt
Assistant Commissioner

Department of The Interior
Office of The Secretary
June 30, 1920

The within will of Chotowizi, deceased Yankton Sioux allottee No. 242, of the Fort Peck Reservation, is hereby approved in accordance with the provisions of the Act of June 25, 1910 (36 Stats. L., 855-6) as amended by Act of February 14, 1913 (37 Stats. L., 678).

SG Hopkins
Assistant Secretary

▲▼▲▼▲▼▲▼▲▼▲▼▲▼

WILLIAM BEAN, SR. *(#1)*

Will of

WILLIAM BEAN, SR.

IN THE NAME OF GOD AMEN.

I, William Bean, Sr., Yankton Sioux Allottee No. 1466, of the State of South Dakota, County of Charles Mix, being of sound and disposing mind, and memory, but being uncertain of life and certain of the approach of death, and desiring to dispose of all my worldly possessions while I still have the power to do so do make and declare this to be my last will and testament hereby revoking and annuling[sic] any and all wills heretofore made by me.

Indian Wills, 1911 – 1921 Book Six
Records of The Bureau of Indian Affairs

First: I bequeath to my son, William Bean, Jr., the sum of Twenty ($20) Dollars;

Second: I bequeath to my daughter, Alma Bean Graycane, the sum of Twenty ($20) Dollars;

Third: I bequeath to my daughter, Susan Bean, the sum of Twenty ($20) Dollars;

Fourth: I bequeath to my daughter, Mary Bean, Jr., the sum of Twenty ($20) Dollars;

Fifth: I bequeath to my beloved wife, Mary Bean, Sr., all the residue of my property both real and personal, after paying all my just debts and funeral expenses, and providing for a suitable monument for my grave.

In testimony whereof, I have set my hand and seal this the 8th day of March, 1917, at Greenwood, the State of South Dakota, County of Charles Mix.

His right
William Bean, Sr. [thumb print]
thumb mark.

Witnesses to mark:
Daniel Brunot - His [thumb print] mark.
Moses Archambeau

Signed, sealed, published and declared this the 8th day of March, 1917, by the said William Bean, Sr., in our presence, as and for his last will and testimony, and at his request and in his presence, and in the presence of each other, we have here unto subscribed our names as attesting witnesses.

(Signature Illegible)   Daniel Brunot - His [thumb print] mark.
Witness to mark of Daniel Brunot   *Moses Archambeau*

Department of The Interior,   JUN 26 1920
Office of Indian Affairs, Washington,
It is hereby recommended that the within will of William Bean, Sr., Yankton Sioux allottee No. 1466, be approved pursuant to the provisions of the Act of June 25, 1910 (36 Stats. L., 855-6) as amended by Act of February 14, 1913 (37 Stats. L., 678).

Respectfully,

EB Meritt

Assistant Commissioner

Department of The Interior

Office of The Secretary JUN 30 1920

The within will of William Bean, Sr., Yankton Sioux allottee No. 1466, is hereby approved pursuant to the provisions of the Act of June 25, 1910 (36 Stats. L., 855-6) as amended by Act of February 14, 1913 (37 Stats. L., 678).

SG Hopkins

Assistant Secretary

▲▼▲▼▲▼▲▼▲▼▲▼▲▼▲▼

ISAAC ZANE

LAST WILL AND TESTAMENT OF ISAAC ZANE.

I, Isaac Zane, of the County of Ottawa and State of Oklahoma, an allottee of the Wyandotte Tribe of Indians, sixty-six years of age, being of sound and disposing mind and realizing my serious ilness[sic] and the frailty of my body, publish and declare this as and for my Last Will and Testament, in manner and form as follows:

First: That all of my just debts and funeral expenses shall be paid.

Second: I give and bequeath the Northeast quarter of the Southeast quarter (NE1/4 of SE1/4) of Section 18 in Township 27 North of Range 24 East of the Indian Meridian, in Oklahoma unto my beloved Wife and my Minor Son, Winnie M. and Joseph Zane to share in share and share alike and unto my five children, namely, Iona, Susie, Louisa, Isaac and Joseph. I give and bequeath the Northwest quarter of the Southwest quarter (NW1/4 of SW1/4) of Section 17 in said Township 27 North of Range 24 East, share and share alike, the above names Joseph Zane to have a one half interest in first above described forty acre tract and a one fifth interest in the second above described forty acre tract for the reason that he is a minor and my youngest child.

IN WITNESS WHEREOF I Have hereunto set my hand and seal in the said County of Ottawa and State of Oklahoma, on this the seventh day of June in the year of Our LORD, 1918.

Isaac Zane (SEAL)

Signed, sealed, published and declared by Isaac Zane, the above named testator, in the presence of us, who at his request, in his presence and in the presence of each other, have hereunto set our names as subscribing and attesting witnesses to the foregoing instrument as the Last Will and Testament of the said Isaac Zane, on this the seventh day of June in the year of Our LORD, One Thousand Nine hundred and Eighteen.

John Bland	of	*Manor, Okla*
(Signature Illegible)	of	*(Residence Illegible)*

Department of The Interior,
Office of Indian Affairs, Washington,
                    JUL 1 1920
It is recommended that the within will of Isaac Zane, Seneca allottee No. 233, be approved under the Act of June 25, 1910 (36 Stats. L., 855-6) as amended by Act of February 14, 1913 (37 Stats. L., 678).

EB Meritt
Assistant Commissioner

Department of The Interior
Office of The Secretary
                    JUL 8- 1920
The within will of Isaac Zane, Seneca allottee No. 233, is approved under the Act of June 25, 1910 (36 Stats. L., 855-6) as amended by Act of February 14, 1913 (37 Stats. L., 678), and the Regulations of the Department.

SG Hopkins
Assistant Secretary

▲▼▲▼▲▼▲▼▲▼▲▼▲▼▲▼

MOSES GILLAM

WILL AND TESTAMENT.
-of-
Moses Gillam, Siletz Allottee No. 174

I, Moses Gillam, Siletz Allottee No. 174, of the Siletz Reservation, Oregon, of lawful age (being about 68 years of age), and being of sound and disposing mind and memory, do hereby make, publish, and declare this to be my last will and testament, hereby revoking all former wills by me made:

FIRST:- I give and devise my original allotment on the Siletz Reservation No. 174, described as the SW/4 of NE/4, and NW/4 of SE/4 or the Lots numbered 13, 14, 19 and 20, of Sec. 36, T. 6, S, R. 11 W., W.M., in Oregon, containing 80 acres, and also all of my inherited allotment No. 175, which I inherited from my prior deceased wife, Louisa Gilliam, or Louisa Gillam, or Lucy Gillam, deceased Siletz Allottee No. 175, which consists of 80 acres of land on the Siletz Reservation in the State of Oregon, in equal shares to William Dick, and Joseph Dick, both of Devils Lake, Oregon. It being my intention to give each the said William Dick and the said Joseph Dick an equal interest in all of my trust lands, both original and inherited interests.

SECOND: I give, devise, and bequeath all the rest and residue of any property of whatsover[sic] nature, either real, personal or mixed, including all inherited interests, of which I may be possessed or entitled to at the time of my death, in equal shares to the said William Dick, and the said Joseph Dick. It being my intention to make these two persons my only beneficiaries under this will, each taking an equal share in the whole of my property.

WITNESS my HAND and SEAL, this NINTH day of OCTOBER, 1918, at the home of Henry Johnson, near the Siletz Agency, Oregon.

WITNESSES TO MARK: His

F M Carter , Physician   MOSES GILLAM.

A J Cassidy , Examiner   mark.

The foregoing instrument, signed, sealed, and acknowledged by said testator as and for his last will and testament in our presence, who at his request, in his presence, and in the presence of each other, have subscribed our names as witnesses thereto this NINTH day of OCTOBER, 1918.

AJ Cassidy
Examiner of Inheritance.

Edwin L Chaleroff   *F M Carter, M.D.*
SUPERINTENDENT.   PHYSICIAN

Department of The Interior,
Office of Indian Affairs, Washington,

JUN 25 1920

It is recommended that the within will of Moses Gillam, Siletz allottee No. 174, be approved under the Act of June 25, 1910 (36 Stats. L., 855-6) as amended by Act of February 14, 1913 (37 Stats. L., 678).

EB Meritt
Assistant Commissioner

Department of The Interior
Office of The Secretary

JUN 30 1920

The within will of Moses Gillam, Siletz allottee No. 174, is hereby approved under the Act of June 25, 1910 (36 Stats. L., 855-6) as amended by Act of February 14, 1913 (37 Stats. L., 678), and the Regulations of the Department.

SG Hopkins
Assistant Secretary

▲▼▲▼▲▼▲▼▲▼▲▼▲▼

HATTIE GEORGE

WILL

IN THE NAME OF GOD, AMEN: I, **Hattie George** age **23**, an Indian of the Nez Perce Indian Reservation, Idaho, now residing at **Spalding** Idaho, being of sound mind and disposing memory, and not acting under duress, menace, fraud, or undue influence, of any person whatsoever, do hereby make, publish and declare this my LAST WILL AND TESTAMENT, in the manner following, that is to say:

First: I direct that my body be decently buried with proper regard to my station in life, and the circumstances of my estate.
Second: I direct that my funeral expenses and expenses of my last illness be paid from any funds belonging to my estate, or in the custody of the Superintendent of the Nez Perce Indian Reservation, Lapwai, Idaho.

Third: I will and bequeath to **Thomas Reuben, with whom I have been living for about one year as common law wife**, the sum of **Three Hundred Dollars ($300)** cash, to be paid from proceeds sale of my interest in allotment 1746 of Titus Amos George, whenever said sale is approved by the Secretary of the Interior.

Fourth: To Lucy Paul, my niece, I will and bequeath whatever cash balance shall remain to the credit of my estate, also my one half interest in allotment 1745 of Te ya se ma, described as Lot 4, SW1/4, NE1/4, NW1/4, SE1/4, and N1/2N1/2S1/2SE1/4, all of section 33 twp. 37 N. R 2 W; also any other property with which I may be possessed at the time of my death.

In witness whereof, I have hereunto put my hand and seal this **11** day of **April 1919**

Her

Hattie George [thumb print]

mark

The foregoing instrument was on the date hereof signed, sealed, published and declared by said **Hattie George** to be **her** LAST WILL AND TESTAMENT, in the presence of us, and at **her** request and in **her** presence, and in the presence of each other, we have subscribed our names as witnesses on this **11** day of **April 1919**.

W. N. Siekels

Francis McFarland

Edith Simpson

Department of The Interior,
Office of Indian Affairs, Washington,
JUN 18 1920

The within will of Hattie George, deceased unallotted Nez Perce Indian, is respectfully recommended for approval pursuant to the provisions of the Act of June 25, 1910 (36 Stats. L., 855-6) as amended by Act of February 14, 1913 (37 Stats. L., 678).

EB Meritt

Assistant Commissioner

Department of The Interior
Office of The Secretary JUN 30 1920

The within will of Hattie George, deceased unallotted Nez Perce Indian, is hereby approved pursuant to the provisions of the Act of June 25, 1910

(36 Stats. L., 855-6) as amended by Act of February 14, 1913 (37 Stats. L., 678).

SG Hopkins
Assistant Secretary

▲▼▲▼▲▼▲▼▲▼▲▼▲▼▲▼

HENRY FASTHORSE

WILL

IN THE NAME OF GOD AMEN:

I, **Henry Fasthorse** Fort Peck allottee No. **324** residing at **Brockton**, Montana, being of sound mind but of feeble health and realizing the uncertainty of life, and not acting under fraud, duress, menace or undue influence, do this **12** day of **July**, 1919, make, publish and declare the following to be my last will and testament:

First:
I give, devise and bequeath
to my beloved wife Lot 4 -Sec 6 - 27-52 5*3*
being my irrigable allotment on the Fort Peck Reservation. Also a team harness and wagon, the team to be a sorrel mare and a blue horse. Also all the money now to my credit or to my credit at the time of my death at the Ft. Peck Agency Office after the payment of my funeral expenses.

Second, I give, devise and bequeath

to my son Geo. Fasthorse the SE of NW and S Half of SW of NE of Section 11 27-52. Also the new set of harness and a roan horse. Also a one half interest in in[sic] my timber allotment Lot 9, 13-27-52, also my machinery consisting of a plow and harrow.

Third:
I give, devise and bequeath **my son Britton Fasthorse the yearling and a sucking colt belonging to the sorrel mare and a one half interest in the timber allotment described as Lot 9-13-27-52**

Fourth, I give devise and bequeath to my four children, share and share alike all moneys not yet paid into the Fort Peck Agency Office

at the time of my death on land sale No. M 3, being the sale of a part of my allotment. Also my share of the estate of my deceased son John Fasthorse.

Fifth,
I give devise and bequeath to my wife and four children share and share alike any property that may accrue to my estate, not above enumerated either before or subsequent to my death.

I hereby appoint E. D. Mossman, Supt. of Fort Peck Agency, or his successor in office, as executor of my estate.

His
Henry Fasthorse [thumb print]
Fort Peck allottee No. **324** *mark*

Witness:
Burton F Roth
Don Mitchell
Witness to signature and Interpreter.

We, the undersigned, hereby certify on our honor that neither of us are related in any way to the testattor[sic], that we were both present and witnessed the signature of the testattor[sic] to the above instrument in one page which **he** read and fully understood before signing as **he** was apparently of sound mind and signed the same of **his** own free will and accord stating that **his** wishes were duly set forth.

Burton F Roth
James F Smith

Department of The Interior,
Office of Indian Affairs, Washington,
JUN 18 1920
The within will of Herny[sic] Fast Horse, deceased Fort Peck Yankton Sioux allottee No. 324, of the Fort Peck Reservation, is recommended for approval in accordance with the provisions of the Act of June 25, 1910 (36 Stats. L., 855-6) as amended by Act of February 14, 1913 (37 Stats. L., 678).

Respectfully,
EB Meritt
Assistant Commissioner

Department of The Interior
Office of The Secretary *June 30/20*

The within will of Henry Fast Horse, deceased Fort Peck Yankton Sioux allottee No. 324, of the Fort Peck Reservation, is hereby approved in accordance with the provisions of the Act of June 25, 1910 (36 Stats. L., 855-6) as amended by Act of February 14, 1913 (37 Stats. L., 678).

> *SG Hopkins*
> Assistant Secretary

▲ ▼ ▲ ▼ ▲ ▼ ▲ ▼ ▲ ▼ ▲ ▼ ▲ ▼ ▲

TAUP-BOODLE

OFFICE OF INDIAN AFFAIRS
RECEIVED
OCT 17 1918
84081

LAST WILL AND TESTAMENT

Anadarko, Oklahoma,
October 9, 1918

I, Taup-boodle, Kiowa allottee No. 683, of Ft Cobb, Caddo County, Oklahoma, 65 years of age, sound of body and mind, but sensible of the uncertainty of life and desiring to make disposition of my property and affairs, while in health and strength, do hereby make, publish and declare the following to be my last will and testament, hereby revoking and cancelling all other or former wills by me at any time made.

1. I direct the payment of all of my just debts and funeral expenses.

2. I give and devise all of my property, real and personal of which I may die possessed to the following persons, in equal shares:

 a. to my beloved husband, Ta-ne-tone, Kiowa allottee No. 2682, one-half of all of my said property.

 b. to my beloved Grand-son, George Tane-tone (Zoam) Kiowa alllottee[sic] No. 684, one-half of my said property.

The above devises are to include the North-half of the North East of 14-6N-12, being the remainder of my trust allotment of land remaining unsold.

Were I to die intestate my property would pass to the above named beneficiaries in the same shares as shown herein, they being my sold[sic] heirs at law at the present time.

This will is made subject to the approval of the Secretary of the Interior.

IN WITNESS WHEREOF, I, Taup-boodle have to this my last will and testament consisting of two sheets of paper, subscribe[sic] my name this 9th day of October, 1918, at Kiowa Indian Agency, Anadarko, Oklahoma.

her
Taup-boodle [thumb print]
mark

Witnesses:
Bertha Higdon
Mary Moulden

Subscribed by Taup-boodle in the presence of each of us, the undersigned, and at the same time declared by her to us to be her last will and testament, and we thereupon, at the request of Taup-boodle in her presence and in the presence of each other, sign our names hereto as witnesses this 9th day of October, 1918, at Kiowa Indian Agency, Anadarko, Oklahoma.

Bertha Higdon
Anadarko, Okla P.O.
Mary Moulden
Anadarko, Okla P.O.

INTERPRETER'S CERTIFICATE

I, Jasper Saunkeah, hereby certify on honor that I acted as interpreter during the execution of the foregoing last will and testament by Taup--boodle; that I interpreted fully and correctly all of the contents thereof before it was executed by her, and that said will was drawn strictly in accordance with her desires and directions. I further certify that I have no interest in this matter whatsoever, and that I speak both the Kiowa Indian, as well as the English Languages fluently.

Signed this 9th day of October, 1918.

Jasper Saunkeah
Interpreter.

Department of The Interior,
Office of Indian Affairs, Washington, JUN 28 1920

It is hereby recommended that the within will of Taup-boodle, deceased Kiowa allottee No. 683, be approved in accordance with the provisions of the Act of June 25, 1910 (36 Stats. L., 855-6) as amended by Act of February 14, 1913 (37 Stats. L., 678), and the Regulations of the Department, but no rights of an executor will be recognized.

Respectfully,
EB Meritt
Assistant Commissioner

Department of The Interior
Office of The Secretary JUN 30 1920

The within will of Taup-boodle, deceased Kiowa allottee No. 683, is hereby approved in accordance with the provisions of the Act of June 25, 1910 (36 Stats. L., 855-6) as amended by Act of February 14, 1913 (37 Stats. L., 678), and the Regulations of the Department, but no rights of an executor will be recognized.

SG Hopkins
Assistant Secretary

KEI-KEI-QUOOT (GAW-KY)

OFFICE OF INDIAN AFFAIRS
RECEIVED
NOV 1- 1918
87887

LAST WILL AND TESTAMENT.

Carnegie, Oklahoma,
Oct. 10 , 1918

I, Kei-kei-quoot, (Gaw-ky) Kiowa allottee No. 242, of Carnegie, Caddo County, Oklahoma, being now in good health, strength of body and mind, but sensible of the uncertainty of life, and desiring to make disposition of my property and affairs, while in health and strength, do hereby make, publish and declare the following to be my last will and testament, hereby revoking and cancelling all other or former wills by me at any time made.

1. I direct the payment of all my just debts and funeral expenses.

2. I give and devise all of my property, real and personal, of which I may die possessed, including my trust allotment of land, comprising the Fractional South West Quarter, Section 19, Township 7 North, Range 12 West of the Indian Meridian, known upon the rolls of the Interior Department, as Kiowa allotment No. 242, to the following beneficiaries, in equal shares:

a. To Tah-lo (Lone Bear) Kiowa allottee No. 690, my son, one-fourth.

b. A-taddle-ty (Joe) Kiowa allottee No. 2478, my son, one-fourth.

c. To E-pay-bo, Kiowa allottee No. 247, my daughter, one-fourth.

d. To Mips-au-tay, an unallotted Kiowa Indian, my grand daughter, one-fourth.

In the event that I should die intestate, my property would pass to the following persons who constitute my sold[sic] heirs, as far as I can determine:

a. Tah-lo, Kiowa allottee No. 690, my son

b. A-taddle-ty Kiowa allottee No. 2478, my son

c. E-pay-bo, Kiowa allottee No. 247, my daughter

I have high regard for my grand daughter Mips Au-tay[sic], have received many favors at her hand, and I have decided, with the consent and approval of all of the heirs at law, to bestow upon her one-fourth of my property to take effect upon my death.

This will is made subject to the approval of the Secretary of the Interior.

In Witness Whereof, I Kei-kei-quoot, have to this my last will and testament, consiting[sic] of two sheets of paper, subscribe my name this *10* day of *Oct* 1918,   *Her*

Kei-kei-quoot [thumb print]
thumb mark

Subscribed by Kei-kei-quoot, in the presence of each of us, the undersigned, and at the same time, declared by him to us to he his last will and testament, and we, thereupon, at the request of Kei-kei-quoot, in his presence and in the presence of each other, sign our names hereto as witnesses this **10** day of **Oct**, 1918, at Carnegie, in Caddo County, Oklahoma.

Matthew Botane
Carnegie, Okla. P.O.
M.A. Claypool
Carnegie, Okla P.O.

INTERPRETER'S CERTIFICATE.

I, *Matthew Botane* hereby certify on honor that I acted as interpreter during the execution of the foregoing last will and testament by Kei-kei-quoot; that I interpreted truthfully and fully all of the contents of said will to the testator before he executed the same, and that all of the devises therein contained met with his full approval and consent, and that said will was drawn strictly in accordance with his desires and directions. I further certify that I speak both the Kiowa Indian, as well as the English languages fluently, and that I have no interest in this matter whatsoever.

Signed this *10* day of *Oct*, 1918.

Matthew Botane
Interpreter

HEIR'S WAIVER.

We, Tah-lo, Kiowa allottee No. 690, A-taddle-ty (Joe) Kiowa allottee No. 2478, and E-pay-bo, Kiowa allottee No. 247, being the heirs at law of Kei-kei-quoot, Kiowa allottee No. 242, hereby consent to the approval of the within will by Kei-kei-quoot. We have had read to us the provisions of the foregoing will, know the contents thereof, and know that we have been partially disinherited in order to grant, or bestow, upon Mips- Au-tay, a share of Kei-kei-quoot's estate. We, and each of us, hereby waive all of our rights that we at law have to so much of the property as is to be bestowed upon Mips Au-tay, and join in the request of Kei-kei-quoot for the approval of said instrument.

Signed this *10* day of *Oct* , 1918.

Witnesses:

                                      His
               Tah lo [thumb print]
M.A. Claypool   *thumb mark*
Matthew Botane

                                      Her
        A taddle-ty [thumb print]
M.A. Claypool   *thumb mark*
Matthew Botane

                                      Her
        E pay-bo [thumb print]
M.A. Claypool   *thumb mark*
Matthew Botane

Department of the Interior,
Office of Indian Affairs, Washington,

JUN 29 1920

It is recommended that the within will of Kei kei quoot (Gaw-ky), be approved in accordance with the Act of June 25, 1910 (36 Stats. L. 855-6) as amended by Act of February 14, 1913 (37 Stats. L. 678), and the Regulations of the Department.

                          Respectfully,
                          EB Meritt
                          Assistant Commissioner

Department of The Interior
Office of The Secretary, Washington
          JUN 30 1920

The within will of Kei kei quoot (Gaw-ky), is hereby approved in accordance with the provisions of the Act of June 25, 1910 (36 Stats. L. 855-6) as amended by Act of February 14, 1913 (37 Stats. L. 678), and the Regulations of the Department.

                          SG Hopkins
                          Assistant Secretary

▲▼▲▼▲▼▲▼▲▼▲▼▲▼

MARY BLAKE

OFFICE OF INDIAN AFFAIRS
RECEIVED
SEP 24 1919
81517

IN THE NAME OF GOD, AMEN. I, Mary Blake of the county of Ravalli, State of Montana, of the age of about 80 years, and being of sound and disposing mind and memory and not acting under duress, fraud, or undue influence of any person or persons whatsoever, do make publish and declare this to be my last will and testament in manner following, that is to say:

FIRST: I direct that my body be decently buried with proper regard to my station in life and the circumstances of my estate.

SECOND: I direct that all my just debts be paid.

THIRD: I give, devise and bequeath to my five children, Namely: Julia Blake Yates, Anna Blake Reed, John Blake, Edward Blake and Bertha Blake Rowan, all the property of which I die possessed, both real and personal wheresoever situated. Property to be shared equally. that is, each to receive one/fifth.

And I hereby appoint J.J. Bond if Victor, Montana, executor of this my last will and testament, hereby revoking all other former wills made by me.

IN WITNESS WHEREOF, I have hereunto set my hand this 20th day of February, 1919.

her
Mary   X   Blake
mark

Rose Ann Ess
    Witness to the mark of Mary Blake
Stanley Waylett
    Witness to the mark of Mary Blake

The foregoing instrument consisting of one page only was on this date hereof, by the said Mary Blake, signed sealed and published[sic] as and declared to be her last will and testament in the presence of us, who at her request and in her presence and in the presence of each other have subscribed our names as witnesses thereto.

Residing at Victor, Montana	H.C. Croff
Residing at Victor, Montana	Stanley Waylett
" " " "	RoseAnn Ess

STATE OF MONTANA :
                   : SS
COUNTY OF RAVALLI :

I, J.T. Coughenour, clerk of the District Court

of the Fourth Judicial District of the State of Montana, in and for Ravalli County do hereby certify that the foregoing is a true and correct copy of the will of Mary Blake on file in my office and duly admitted to probate by the District Court of the Fourth Judicial District of the State of Montana, in and for Ravalli County.

WITNESS, my hand and the seal of said court this 20th day of August, 1919.

J.T. Coughenour
Clerk

Department of The Interior,
Office of Indian Affairs, Washington,
MAY -6 1920

The within will of Mary Blake, deceased Public Domain allottee No. 22 of the Snake tribe, is respectfully recommended for approval pursuant to the provisions of the Act of June 25, 1910 (36 Stats. L., 855-6) as amended by Act of February 14, 1913 (37 Stats. L., 678).

EB Meritt
Assistant Commissioner

Department of The Interior
Office of The Secretary MAY -7 1920

The within will of Mary Blake, deceased Public Domain allottee No. 22 of the Snake tribe, is hereby approved pursuant to the provisions of the Act of June 25, 1910 (36 Stats. L., 855-6) as amended by Act of February 14, 1913 (37 Stats. L., 678).

SG Hopkins
Assistant Secretary

▲▼▲▼▲▼▲▼▲▼▲▼▲▼

JOSEPH POWELL
LAST WILL AND TESTAMENT
OF
JOSEPH POWELL
Devils Lake Allottee No. 655

I, Joseph Powell, being of sound mind, memory and understanding, and not being under compulsion or any stress of circumstances, do hereby make, publish and declare this my last Will and

Testament, hereby revoking and annulling all wills by me heretofore made, in manner and form following, that is to say:

First - I direct that all my just debts and funeral expenses *and* of my last illness shall be paid by my wife, Jennie Powell, and my daughter, Julia Blueshield, from any funds that may come from my estate.

Second - To my wife, Jennie Powell, I give and bequeath that portion of my allotment described as Lots 4, 5, and 6, Sec 17, T 151, R. 63, containing 73.30 acres.

To my son, Francis Powell, I give and bequeath that portion of my allotment described as the SW/4 of the SE/4 of Sec. 17, T. 151, R. 63.

To my daughter, Julia Blueshield, I give and bequeath that portion of my allotment described as the NW/4 of the NE/4 (Lot 2), and the SE/4 of the NE/4 of Sec. 1, T. 151, R. 64, containing 53.72 acres, including the improvements thereon.

Third - I do hereby nominate, constitute and appoint Iyapawaste, or Gideon Smith, as executor of this my last will and testament.

IN TESTIMONY WHEREOF, I have set my hand and seal to this, my last Will and Testament, at Tokio, N. Dak., this 11th day of July, in the year of our Lord 1918, in the presence of S.A.M. Young and Wm Maxwell, Jr., who at my request and in my presence are signing as witnesses, we all signing in the presence of each other.

Joseph Powell

Signed, Sealed, Published and Declared by the said Joseph Powell in our presence, as and for his last Will and Testament, and at his request and in our presence, and in the presence of each other, we have hereunto subscribed our names as attesting witnesses thereto.

S.A.M Young
Wm. Maxwell, Jr.

Department of The Interior,
Office of Indian Affairs, Washington,

MAY -3 1920

It is recommended that the within will be approved pursuant to the provisions of the Act of June 25, 1910 (36 Stats. L., 855-6) as amended by Act of February 14, 1913 (37 Stats. L., 678).

Respectfully,
EB Meritt
Assistant Commissioner

Department of The Interior
Office of The Secretary   MAY 17 1920

The within will is hereby approved pursuant to the provisions of the Act of June 25, 1910 (36 Stats. L., 855-6) as amended by Act of February 14, 1913 (37 Stats. L., 678), and the Regulations of the Department.

SG Hopkins
Assistant Secretary

▲ ▼ ▲ ▼ ▲ ▼ ▲ ▼ ▲ ▼ ▲ ▼ ▲ ▼

JOSEPH GARNEAUX, SR.

77-Short Will   Ex "Ä"   Guffman's General Supply
House, York, Nebraska.

IN THE NAME OF GOD, AMEN.

I, Joseph Garneaux, Sr., of Wood, S.D. in the County of Mellette, State of South Dakota, being of sound mind and memory, and considering the uncertainty of this frail and transitory life, do therefore make, ordain, publish and declare this to be my last WILL AND TESTAMENT:

FIRST, I order and direct that my Executor hereinafter named, pay all my just debts and funeral expenses as soon after my decease as conveniently may be.

SECOND, After the payment of such funeral expenses and debts, I give, devise and bequeath to my son, Edward Garneaux, all my horses that at the time of my death are broken to drive or ride, also one lumber wagon, two sets of work harness, one open buggy, and all farming implements. It is my desire that the balance of my belongings be divided equally between my four children, viz: Edward, Joseph, Ambrose, and Josephine.

LASTLY, I make, constitute and appoint Edward Garneaux to be Executor of this my last Will and Testament, hereby revoking all former wills by me made.

IN WITNESS WHEREOF, I have hereunto subscribed my name and affixed my seal, the 19th day of January in the year of our Lord, one thousand nine hundred fourteen.

(signed) Joseph Garneaux, Sr. Seal

This Instrument was on the day of the date thereof, signed, published and declared by the said testator Joseph Garneaux, Sr., to be his last Will and Testament, in the presence of us who at his request have subscribed our names thereto as witnesses in his presence and in the presence of each other.

(Signed)   G. L. Watson
(Signed)   M. M. Watson

I hereby certify this 16th day of September, 1919, that the foregoing is a true and correct copy of the will of Joseph Garneaux, Sr., filed in the County Court of Mellette County, State of South Dakota, on the 12th day of July, 1919.

Joseph Coursey
Examiner of Inheritance

Department of The Interior,
Office of Indian Affairs, Washington,
MAY -4 1920

It is hereby recommended that the within will of Joseph Garneau[sic], Sr., deceased Rosebud Sioux allottee No. 367, be approved under the provisions of the Act of June 25, 1910 (36 Stats. L., 855-6) as amended by Act of February 14, 1913 (37 Stats. L., 678), and the Regulations of the Department.

Respectfully,
EB Meritt
Assistant Commissioner

Department of The Interior
Office of The Secretary   MAY 18 1920

The within will of Joseph Garneau[sic], Sr., deceased Rosebud Sioux allottee No. 367, is hereby approved under the provisions of the Act of June 25, 1910 (36 Stats. L., 855-6) as amended by Act of February 14, 1913 (37 Stats. L., 678), and the Regulations of the Department.

SG Hopkins
Assistant Secretary

▲▼▲▼▲▼▲▼▲▼▲▼▲▼▲▼

WILLIAM STEALS THE BEAR

Last Will and Testament
of
William Steals The Bear

OFFICE OF INDIAN AFFAIRS
RECEIVED
JUL 7- 1919
57837

IN THE NAME OF GOD, AMEN.

I, **William Steals The Bear** of **Lodge Grass, Montana**, being of sound mind, memory, and understanding, do hereby make and publish this my last will and testament, hereby revoking and annulling all wills by me heretofore made, in manner and form following, that is to say:

First; I direct that all my just debts and funeral expenses, and expenses of my last illness shall be paid by my executor hereinafter named as soon after my decease as convenient;
Second; I give, devise and bequeath to

Kitty Medicine Tail (Mrs. Deer Nose) my disc plow, all my interest in all land on Gros Ventre reservation, all money anywhere to my credit, all my own land and all my interest in all other lands or tribal holdings, except my share in the 40 acres of Sings Around The Hoop at Hardin, Montana, which I give to Media Blaine, and my share in the grazing land of Sings Around The Hoop, which I give to Joe Not Afraid,
To Blake White Man - One grey *horse* (with his own brand) and my disc harrow,
To Packs The Hat - One buckskin mare, one black gelding branded 4-

To Ben Spotted Horse - One grey mare branded 4-
To Medcine[sic] Crow - one old Mitchell lumber wagon
To Plenty Hawks - One cream colored mare, branded 4-
To Mrs. Ben Spotted Horse - One ball-faced mare, branded 4-
To Joe Not Afraid - Set work harness, new Scheuttler Wagon
To Mrs. Packs The Hat - One bay mare, branded 4-
To Kitty Medicine Tail (Mrs. Deer Nose) all the rest of my personal property

Third; All the rest and residue of my estate, both real, and personal and mixed, I give devise and bequeath to my lawful heirs as determined after my decease.

And lastly; I do hereby nominate, constitute and appoint **C.H. Asbury, Supt. or successor** executor of this my last will and testament.

In testimony Whereof, I have set my hand and seal to this, my last will and testament, at **Lodge Grass** Montana, this **fifth** day of **March**, in the year of our Lord one thousand nine hundred and **nineteen**.

His
William Steals The Bear [thumb print]
mark.

Signed, sealed, published and declared by said **William Steals The Bear** in our presence, as and for **his** last Will and testament, and at **his** request and in our presence, and in the presence of each other, we have hereunto subscribed our names as attesting witnesses thereto.

SP Cope	of	**Lodge Grass, Montana**
William H (Illegible)	of	**Lodge Grass, Montana**
George Hill	of	**Lodge Grass, Montana**

Department of The Interior,
Office of Indian Affairs, Washington,

JUN 24 1920

It is hereby recommended that the within will of William Steals The Bear, deceased Crow allottee No. 1031, be approved under the provisions of the Act of June 25, 1910 (36 Stats. L., 855-6) as amended by Act of February 14, 1913 (37 Stats. L., 678), and the Regulations of the Department.

Respectfully,
EB Meritt
Assistant Commissioner

Department of The Interior
Office of The Secretary   JUN 30 1920

The within will of William Steals The Bear, deceased Crow allottee No. 1031, is hereby approved under the provisions of the Act of June 25, 1910 (36 Stats. L., 855-6) as amended by Act of February 14, 1913 (37 Stats. L., 678), and the Regulations of the Department.

SG Hopkins
Assistant Secretary

▲▼▲▼▲▼▲▼▲▼▲▼▲▼▲▼

WILLIAM BEAN, SR. (#2)

WILL OF WILLIAM BEAN, SR.

IN THE NAME OF GOD AMEN.

I, William Bean, Sr., Yankton Sioux Allottee No. 1466, of the State of South Dakota, County of Charles Mix, being of sound and disposing mind, and memory, but being uncertain of life and certain of the approach of death, and desiring to dispose of all my worldly possessions while I still have the power to do so do make and declare this to be my last will and testament hereby revoking and annuling[sic] any and all wills heretofore made by me.

First; It is my will that my present wife Mary Bean Sr. with whom I have lived for over sixty years, shall have the exclusive use and possession of all of my allotment No. 1466 on the Yankton Sioux Reservation during the remainder of her life should she survive me.

Second; It is my will that upon the death of my wife Mary Bean Sr. that portion of my allotment described as lot 293 according according[sic] to the survey of the Yankton reservation, shall be given to my daughter Mary Bean Jr.

Third; It is my will that upon the death of my wife Mary Bean Sr. that portion of my allotment described as lot 294 according to the survey of the Yankton reservation, be given to my daughter Susan Bean.

Fourth; It is my will that upon the death of my wife Mary Bean Sr. that portion of my allotment described as lot 299 according to the survey of the Yankton reservation be given to my daughter Alma Bean.

Fifth; It is my will that upon the death of my wife Mary Bean Sr. that that portion of my allotment describer[sic] as lot 300 according to the survey of the Yankton reservation be given to my son William Bean Sr.[sic].

In testimony whereof, I have set my hand and seal this 13th day of January, 1916, at Greenwood, Charles Mix Co, So. Dak.

	His
Wittnesses[sic] to mark	William Bean Sr. [thumb print]
John Picotte	Mark
J B Cournoyer	

Signed, sealed, published and declared this the 13th day of Jan, 1916, by the said William Bean, Sr., in our presence, as and for his last will and testimony, and at his request and in his presence, and in the presence of each other, we have here unto subscribed our names as attesting witnesses.

John Picotte
J B Cournoyer

Department of The Interior,
Office of Indian Affairs, Washington,
AUG -4 1916

The within will of William Bean Sr., Yankton Sioux allottee No. 1488, is hereby recommended for approval under the provisions of the Act of June 25, 1910 (36 Stats. L., 855-6) as amended by Act of February 14, 1913 (37 Stats. L., 678).

Respectfully,
EB Meritt
Assistant Commissioner

Department of The Interior
Office of The Secretary AUG 26 1916

The within will of William Bean Sr., Yankton Sioux allottee No. 1488, is hereby approved in accordance with the Act of June 25, 1910 (36 Stats. L., 855-6) as amended by Act of February 14, 1913 (37 Stats. L., 678).

Bo Sweeney
Assistant Secretary

PROBATE
50269-1916
99460-1919
L L

Department of The Interior
Office of The Secretary   JUN 30 1920

The cancellation of the within will is hereby approved, in view of the fact that the testator executed another will under date of March 8, 1917, which has been approved.

SG Hopkins
Assistant Secretary

▲▼▲▼▲▼▲▼

JENNIE DAVID

State of Oregon)
) SS   Klamath Indian School,
County of Klamath)

RECEIVED OCT 30 1918 87488

RECEIVED OCT 27 1916 112253

Klamath Agency, Oregon.

LAST WILL AND TESTAMENT OF JENNIE DAVID, KLAMATH

INDIAN ALLOTTEE, NO. 119.

I, Jennie David, Allottee No. 119, of the Klamath Indian Reservation, in the County of Klamath, of the State of Oregon, my allotment being still held under trust by the United States, being of sound mind and memory, do hereby make, publish, and declare, this, my last will, in manner and form as follows, that is to say:

First. I direct the payment of all my just debts and funeral expenses, which may be paid under the laws and regulations of the United States.

Second. I give, devise, and bequeath my allotment on the Klamath Reservation in Oregon, consisting of the following described land:- Lots 9, 10, 15 and 16, Section 18, Township 35, Range 7, and Lots 15, 16, 19 and 20, Section 19, Township 35, Range 7 - 160 acres, and all other real property, wherever situate, or any interest therein, of which I may die possessed, or to which I may be entitled, together with all personal property, of whatsoever kind the same may be, which I may own at my death, or in which I may have any interest, to my Grandson, Benjamin Tupper, to have and to hold the same to the said Benjamin Tupper, forever, and his heirs.

Third. I hereby revoke any and all former will by me made.

Fourth. In witness whereof, I have hereunto set my hand and seal, this 6th day of March, 1915, at the Klamath Agency, Oregon.

Her
JENNIE DAVID [thumb print]
Mark.

The foregoing instrument, consisting of 1 page, was at the date hereof, by the said Jennie David signed, sealed and published as, and declared to be, her last will and testament, in the presence of us, who, at her request and in her presence, and in the presence of each other, have subscribed our names as witnesses hereto.

Fred A Baker	residing at	*Klamath Agency, Ore*
Rose Wright	residing at	*Klamath Agency, Ore*
Lulu Lang	residing at	*Klamath Agency, Ore*

Department of The Interior,
Office of Indian Affairs, Washington,
JAN 16 1917

The within will, dated March 6, 1916, of Jennie David, Klamath allottee No. 119, is hereby recommended for approval in pursuance of the Act of June 25, 1910 (36 Stats. L., 855-6) as amended by Act of February 14, 1913 (37 Stats. L., 678).

Respectfully,
EB Meritt
Assistant Commissioner

Department of The Interior
Office of The Secretary   JAN 17 1917

The within will of Jennie David, Klamath allottee No. 119, is hereby approved in pursuance of the Act of June 25, 1910 (36 Stats. L., 855-6) as amended by Act of February 14, 1913 (37 Stats. L., 678).

Bo Sweeney
Assistant Secretary

LUCY BIG OWL

Original
WILL

OFFICE OF INDIAN AFFAIRS
RECEIVED
MAY 10 1915
52127

I, **Lucy Big Owl** of Pine Ridge Agency, South Dakota, Allottee number **6851** do hereby make and declare this to be my last will and testament, in accordance with Section 2 of the Act of June 25, 1910, (36 stat. 855-858) and Act of February 14, 1913, (Public No. 381), hereby revoking all former wills made by me:

1. I hereby direct that as soon as possible after my decease, that all my debts, funeral and testamentary expenses be paid out of my personal estate.

2. I give and devise my allotment on the Pine Ridge Reservation, South Dakota, described as follows:

The South half of Section 20, Township 38, North, of Range 42, West of the Sixth Principal Meridian, South Dakota, containing Three hundred twenty acres.

in the following manner:

To my son Thomas Big Owl, the South East quarter of Section 20, Township 38, North of Range 42, West of the Sixth Principal Meridian, South Dakota, containing One hundred sixty acres.

3. I give and bequeath all of my personal property of whatsoever nature and wheresoever situated unto **Big Owl, my husband, and to Thomas Big Owl, my son.**

4. All the rest of my property, real or personal, now possessed or

hereafter acquired, of whatsoever nature and wheresoever situated, I hereby give, devise and bequeath unto **Big Owl, my husband, and to Thomas Big Owl, my son.**

In witness whereof I have hereunto set my hand this **26th** day of **April** 1915   *her mark*
                                                                                        Lucy Big Owl [thumb print]

The above statement was, this **26th** day of **April** 1915 signed and published by **Lucy Big Owl** as **her** last will and testament, in the joint presence of the undersigned, the said **Lucy Big Owl** then being of sound and vigorous mind and free from any constraint or compulsion; whereupon we, being without any interest in the matter other than friendship, and being well acquainted with **her** but not members of **her** family, immediately subscribed our names hereto in the presence of each other and of the said testator, for the purpose of attesting the said will, as **she** requested us to do. And that I, **O. C. Ross** at the testatrix's request, have written **her** name in ink, and that **she** affixed her thumb-mark.

                                                      Post Office Address
OC Ross   **Pine Ridge Agency, S.D.**
Robert H Stelzner   **Pine Ridge Agency, S.D.**

                                                      Pine Ridge, South Dakota.
                                                      April 26, 1915.
I hereby certify that I have fully inquired into the mental competency of the Indian signing the above will; the circumstances attending the execution of the will; the influence that may have induced its execution, and the names of those entitled to share in the estate under the law of descent in South Dakota: reasons for the disposition of the property proposed by the will differing from disposition had the property descended by operation of law.

I respectfully forward this will with the recommendation that it be …..approved.

                                                      John R Brennan
                                                      Supt. & Spl. Disb. Agent.

Department of the Interior,
Office of Indian Affairs, Washington,
                        MAY 19 1915

It is recommended that the within will be approved under the provisions of the Act of June 25, 1910 (36 Stats. L. 855-6) as amended by Act of February 14, 1913 (37 Stats. L. 678).

CF Hawke
Second Assistant Commissioner

Department of The Interior
Office of The Secretary, Washington MAY 20 1915

The within will is hereby approved under the provisions of the Act of June 25, 1910 (36 Stats. L. 855-6) as amended by Act of February 14, 1913 (37 Stats. L. 678).

Bo Sweeney
Assistant Secretary

Department of The Interior
Office of The Secretary, Washington

The within declaration executed April 12, 1930, by Lucy Big Owl, revoking the approved will made by her April 26, 1915, is hereby approved in accordance with the provisions of the Act of June 25, 1910 (36 Stats. L. 855-6) as amended by Act of February 14, 1913 (37 Stats. L. 678),

SG Hopkins
Assistant Secretary

▲▼▲▼▲▼▲▼▲▼▲▼▲▼▲▼

WILLIAM MEAD

LAST WILL AND TESTAMENT OF WILLIAM MEAD.

I, William Mead, Devils Lake Indian, unallotted, being in my right mind and of disposing memory, and not under compulsion or stress of circumstances, hereby make, declare and publish this my last will and testament, to-wit:

FIRST, I will and bequeath to Jacob Onebear, my uncle, all my undivided interest in the estate of my mother Tehiwin, including in particular allotment 710, being the NE1/4 NW1/4 of Section 8 and the NW1/4 NW1/4 of Section 17 - 151 - 84.

SECOND, I will and bequeath to my grandmother Toahewin all my other inherited interests, including the estates of John Mead, brother;

Moses Mead, half brother; Joseph Kecankoyake, allottee 233, my father; Matowanjina, allottee 707, my grandfather; Tiyowastewin, allottee 708, my grandmother; Akicitaduta, allottee 232, my grandfather; and Wicanhpiigegewin, allottee 329, my great-grandmother.

THIRD, I will and bequeath to Toahewin and Jacob Onebear in equal shares any money wich[sic] may be on deposit to my credit with the Superintendent of the Fort Totten School.

AND LASTLY, I nominate, appoint and constitute Jacob Onebear as executor of this my last will and testament, in testimony whereof I affix my hand and seal this 7th day of August, 1918, at Fort Totten, North Dakota in the presence of Martin Strait, Charles E. Coe and S.A.M. Young, who in my presence and at my request are signing as witnesses, we all signing in the presence of each other.

William Mead

We, Martin Strait, Charles E. Coe and S.A.M. Young at the request of William Mead and in his presence hereby witness the signature of William Mead and know this to be his last will and testament, we all signing in the presence of each other.

Martin Strait
Charles E Coe
S.A.M. Young

Department of the Interior,
Office of Indian Affairs, Washington,

MAY 13 1920

It is recommended that the within will of William Mead, deceased unallotted member of the Devils Lake Sioux tribe, be approved under the Act of June 25, 1910 (36 Stats. L. 855-6) as amended by Act of February 14, 1913 (37 Stats. L. 678),

Respectfully,
EB Meritt
Assistant Commissioner

Department of The Interior
Office of The Secretary, Washington

Indian Wills, 1911 – 1921   Book Six
Records of The Bureau of Indian Affairs

The within will of William Mead, deceased unallotted member of the Devils Lake Sioux tribe, is hereby approved under the Act of June 25, 1910 (36 Stats. L. 855-6) as amended by Act of February 14, 1913 (37 Stats. L. 678).

SG Hopkins
Assistant Secretary

▲▼▲▼▲▼▲▼▲▼▲▼▲▼

LOOKS AT WOMAN or MRS. SEES END OF HORN

Will of Mrs Sees End of Horn.

I, Looks At Woman, Allottee #1920, Ft Peck Agency, Mont. aged 52 years, being of sound and disposing mind do make and declare this my last will and testament and wish that at my death my estate shall all be given to my husband Sees End of Horn, allottee 1890, Ft Peck Agency Mont., aged 63 years, except and provided the sum of $100 shall be given to Spotted Bull, Ft Peck Indian allottee #891 and $100 to his wife, Sarah Spotted Bull, aged 54, Ft Peck Indian allottee 892; one hundred dollars to each of these two named, Mr & Mrs Spotted Bull because they have cared for me and kept me these last (2) months while I have been sick.

I have no other relatives than my husband Sees End of Horn named above.

My property is 2 horses, wagon, harness, and 40 acres of land described as NW^4 of NE^4, Sec 4 T 29, R 54 and 320 acres of grazing land described as (No description given for land)

These lands and property being on the Fort Peck Reservation, Sheridan Co, Mont.
Signed this June 2, 1916   her
Drew, Sheridan Co, Mont [thumb print]   *Looks At Woman*
In presence of   r. thumb
Frederick E. Farrell, Brockton, Mont.
Henry Shield   "   "
Interpreted by Henry Shield, Policeman

Brockton, Mont, June 3, 1916
I hereby certify that this is the will of Mrs Sees End of Horn Looks at Woman, drawn by me at her wish and signed in my presence, and in her sound and clear mind as to her property and its disposal.
I recommended its approval.

F.E. Farrell, Farmer

Department of The Interior,
Office of Indian Affairs, Washington,

JUL 1 1920

The within will of Looks at Woman Sees End of Horn, deceased Yankton Sioux allottee No. 1920, of the Fort Peck Reservation, is hereby recommended for approval in accordance with the provisions of the Act of June 25, 1910 (36 Stats. L., 855-6) as amended by Act of February 14, 1913 (37 Stats. L., 678).

Respectfully,
EB Meritt
Assistant Commissioner

Department of The Interior
Office of The Secretary

The within will of Looks at Woman Sees End of Horn, deceased Yankton Sioux allottee No. 1920, of the Fort Peck Reservation, is hereby approved in accordance with the Act of June 25, 1910 (36 Stats. L., 855-6) as amended by Act of February 14, 1913 (37 Stats. L., 678).

SG Hopkins
Assistant Secretary

▲▼▲▼▲▼▲▼▲▼▲▼▲▼

YELLOW IRON RED CROW

WILL

IN THE NAME OF GOD AMEN:

I, **Yellow Iron Red Crow** Fort Peck allottee No. **744** residing at **Poplar**, Montana, being of sound mind but of feeble health and realizing the uncertainty of life, and not acting under fraud, duress, menace or undue influence, do this **30** day of **November**, **1918**, make, publish and declare the following to be my last will and testament:

First:

I give, devise and bequeath **to my beloved daughter Thelma Red Crow War Club** *and John Anderson* **my grazing allotment described as the E1/2 of Sec. 34 -33-48** *equal shares*

Second, I give, devise and bequeath **to my beloved son John Anderson**

the SW1/4 of NW1/4 of sec. 8-27-50.   This being my irrigable allotment.

Third:

I give, devise and bequeath to my beloved husband, Red Crow all my part and portion in the undetermined estate of my deceased son, James Frank RedCrow including my share as shall be hereafter determined in the N1/2 of 32-30-49, and to beloved husband RedCrow all undetermined and unknown property to which I may now may or may[sic]hereafter be declared to be the heir, aside from what is bequeathed in this will.

Fourth:

I give devise and bequeath to my beloved sisters Brings Water Thundering Bear and Good Star no Eye Brow, all my share and portion to which I may be found heir in the irrigable forty (40) belonging to the estate of my deceased son James Frank RedCrow described as the NW1/4 of SW14 of Sec. 8-27-50 share and share alike.

I hereby appoint E. D. Mossman, Supt. of Fort Peck Agency, or his successor in office, as executor of my estate.   *Her*

Yellow Iron Red Crow [thumb print]

Fort Peck allottee No. **744** *mark*

Witness:

Henry P Keller
Richard Benedict

We, the undersigned, hereby certify on our honor that neither of us are related in any way to the testat...., that we were both present and witnessed the signature of the testat.... to the above instrument in one page which ..... read and fully understood before signing as ..... was apparently of sound mind and signed the same of ..... own free will and accord stating that ..... wishes were duly set forth.

Henry P Keller
Richard Benedict

Department of The Interior,
Office of Indian Affairs, Washington,
                 JUL 2 1920

The within will of Yellow Iron Red Crow, deceased Yankton Sioux allottee No. 744, of the Fort Peck Reservation, is hereby recommended for approval in accordance with the provisions of the Act of June 25, 1910 (36 Stats. L., 855-6) as amended by Act of February 14, 1913 (37 Stats. L., 678).

Respectfully,
EB Meritt
Assistant Commissioner

Department of The Interior
Office of The Secretary JUL -3 1920

The within will of Yellow Iron Red Crow, deceased Yankton Sioux allottee No. 744, of the Fort Peck Reservation, is hereby approved in accordance with the Act of June 25, 1910 (36 Stats. L., 855-6) as amended by Act of February 14, 1913 (37 Stats. L., 678).

SG Hopkins
Assistant Secretary

OFFICE OF INDIAN AFFAIRS
RECEIVED
FEB 14 1920
13385

▲▼▲▼▲▼▲▼▲▼▲▼

THOMAS CLAY

LAST WILL AND TESTAMENT OF THOMAS CLAY.

I, Thomas Clay, being of sound mind, strong body and disposing memory and realizing the uncertainties of life, do hereby make, declare and publish this my last will and testament:

1st.   I desire all my debts that are just and right, including my funeral and burial expenses to be paid out of any funds accruing to my estate:

2nd.   I have property as follows:
The S/2 of the SE/4 of Sec. 29 Twp. 26 N., R. 7 E.
and the SW/4 SE/4 of Sec. 11, Twp. 26 N., R. 9 E.
my allotment
I also have a small share in the Sampson Porter allotment which we hope to sell this fall.

3rd.   I give, devise and bequeath the S/2 of the SE/[sic] of Sec. 29 Twp. 26 N, R 7 E/ to my son James Clay: To my son, John Clay, my son Jesse Clay, my son, James Clay and my daughter, Della Clay, I give the SW/4

SE/4 of Sec. 11, Twp. 26 N., R 9 E, each an equal one-fourth share.

4th.   Whatever other property, including the small portion of the Sampson Porter allotment and whatever personal or real property that I should die possessed of, I give, devise and bequeath to my sons, John Clay, Jesse Clay and James Clay and my daughter Della Clay, each an equal share.   His

Thomas Clay [thumb print]
Mark.

The testator at this time signed his name to the above and foregoing instrument in the presence of the undersigned and at the same time declared it to be his last will and testament, and we at his request and in his presence and in the presence of each other do hereby sign our names hereto as attesting witnesses.   *his*
Interpreter: *Gasin Rainbow* [thumb print]
Hugh Hunter   *mark*

Hugh Hunter

Winnebago Agency, Nebr. July 6, 1918.

Department of The Interior,
Office of Indian Affairs, Washington,
                    MAY 20 1920
The within will dated July 5, 1918, of Thomas Clay, deceased Winnebago allottee No. 640, is hereby recommended for approval in accordance with the provisions of the Act of June 25, 1910 (36 Stats. L., 855-6) as amended by Act of February 14, 1913 (37 Stats. L., 678).

CF Hawke
Acting Assistant Commissioner

Department of The Interior
Office of The Secretary   JUN -1 1920

The within will dated July 5, 1918, of Thomas Clay, deceased Winnebago allottee No. 640, is hereby approved in accordance with the Act of June 25, 1910 (36 Stats. L., 855-6) as amended by Act of February 14, 1913 (37 Stats. L., 678).

SG Hopkins
Assistant Secretary

▲▼▲▼▲▼▲▼▲▼▲▼▲▼▲▼

MARY GRIZZLY BEAR KIYALK

WILL

IN THE NAME OF GOD, AMEN:

BE IT REMEMBERED THAT I, MARY GRIZZLY BEAR KIYALK, Flathead allottee number 1732, now a resident of the Flathead Reservation, of Missoula County, Montana, of the age of 80 years, being of sound and disposing mind and memory, and not acting under duress, fraud, or under the influence of any person whatsoever, do make, publish and declare this, my last will and testament, in the following manner, that is to say:

To my beloved husband, Mark Kiyalk, all property of any and every kind of which I may die possessed, and the sum of $940.00, received from the sale of my allotment and deposited to my credit at the office of the Superintendent of the Flathead Agency, Montana, or the amount remaining on deposit to my credit at the time of my death.

In witness whereof I set my hand and seal this *3rd* day of *September*, in the year of our Lord, one thousand nine hundred eighteen.

her
Mary Grizzley[sic] Bear Kiyalk [thumb print]
mark

The foregoing instrument, consisting of this one page, was at the date thereof, signed, sealed, published, and declared to be her last will and testament, in the presence of each of us, who, at her request, and in the presence of each other, have subscribed our names as witnesses hereto.

Edward Lozean	*N.B. M͡cCay*
St. Ignatius, Montana.	St. Ignatius, Montana.

Department of The Interior,
Office of Indian Affairs, Washington,
APR 30 1920

The within will of Mary Grizzley Bear Kiyalk, deceased Flathead allottee No. 1732, is submitted with the recommendation that it be approved according to the Act of June 25, 1910 (36 Stats. L., 855-6) as amended by Act of February 14, 1913 (37 Stats. L., 678).

Respectfully,

EB Meritt

Assistant Commissioner

Department of The Interior

Office of The Secretary JAN 14 1921

The within will of Mary Grizzley Bear Kiyalk, deceased Flathead allottee No. 1732, is hereby approved according to the Act of June 25, 1910 (36 Stats. L., 855-6) as amended by Act of February 14, 1913 (37 Stats. L., 678). It is found that her husband, Mark Kiyalk succeeds to the estate as sole devisee.

SG Hopkins

Assistant Secretary

▲▼▲▼▲▼▲▼▲▼▲▼

HARRY WHITEBIRD

OFFICE OF INDIAN AFFAIRS

RECEIVED

MAR 24 1920

25398

LAST WILL AND TESTAMENT OF
_____HARRY WHITEBIRD_____

I, Harry Whitebird, of Quapaw, Ottawa County, Oklahoma, being of sound mind but sensible of the uncertainty of life, and desiring to make disposition of my property, assetts[sic], affairs and estate, while in full posession[sic] of a sound mind, do hereby make, publish and declare the following to be my last will and testament, hereby revoking and cancelling all other or former wills by me at any time made :-

1. I direct the payment of all my just debts and funeral expenses.

2. I give and devise to my wife, Flora Young Greenback Whitebird, a one-third (1/3) interest and portion, in and to any and all of my property, both real, personal, or mixed n character, and of whatsoever kind, description or character, and of any and all of my assetts[sic], moneys, goods, chattels, rights or choses[sic] in action, real estate, and in all and any kind of property that I own or in which I have any interest, equity or estate, and of which I may die seized.

3. I give and devise to my son, *Robert Anderson Whitebird* a one-third (1.3) interest and portion in and to any and all of my property, both real, personal, or mixed in character, and of whatsoever kind, description or character, and of any and all of my assetts[sic], moneys, goods,

chattels, rights or choses[sic] in action, real estate, and in all and any kind of property that I own or in which I have any interest, equity or estate, and of which I may die seized.

4. I give and devise to my *grand* daughter, *Helen Irene Whitebird*, a one-third (1/3) interest and portion, in and to any and all of my property, both real, personal, or mixed in character, and of whatsoever kind, description or character, and of any and all of my assetts[sic], moneys, goods, chattels, rights or choses[sic] in action, real estate, and in all and any kind of property that I own or in which I have any interest, equity or estate, and of which I may die seized.

5. I hereby appoint and designate *D. C. DeVilliers* of Ottawa County, Oklahoma, sole executor, without bond, of this, my last will and testament.

IN WITNESS WHEREOF, I, Harry Whitebird, have to this my last will and testament, consisting of two sheets of paper with binding sheet, subscribed my name this 5th day of December, 1919.

Harry Whitebird
Testator

Subscribed by Harry Whitebird in the presence of each of us, the undersigned, at the same time said instrument was declared by him to us to be his last will and testament, and we, thereupon, at the request of said Harry Whitebird, in his presence, and in the presence of each other, sign our names hereunto as witnesses this 5th day of December, 1919, in Quapaw, Oklahoma.

C.A. Douthat
Chas McCallum, M.D.   *W.T. Bingham*
Subscribing Witnesses

* *

State of Oklahoma,
             ss   A C K N O W L E D G E M E N T
County of Ottawa.

Before me, the undersigned, a Notary Public in and for the County and state aforesaid, personally appeared, Harry Whitebird, to me well known to be the identical person who executed the above and foregoing instrument to wit, "LAST WILL AND TESTAMENT OF HARRY WHITEBIRD", and he acknowledged to me that he executed the same as his free and voluntary act and deed for the uses and purposes therein set forth.

IN WITNESS WHEREOF I have hereunto set my hand and affixed my Notarial seal this 5th day of December, 1919.

James Miller
Notary Public

My commission expires
October 18, 19*22*

* * * * * * * * * * * *

Land-Quapaw
  Probate
25398-20
  O ' N

Department of The Interior,
Office of Indian Affairs, Washington,

The will of Harry Whitebird, deceased Quapaw allottee 22-25 dated December 5, 1919, is hereby recommended for approval, according to the Act of June 25, 1910 (36 Stats. L., 855-6) as amended by Act of February 14, 1913 (37 Stats. L., 678-9) excepting as to the executor indicated therein and no rights of an executor are recognized. The approval of this will shall not be construed as a relinquishment of, or militate against the supervision of the United States Government over unpartitioned[sic] inherited lands, or those held under restricted fee, devised therein, and the rents, royalties and revenues derived therefore, if such supervision is required by the status of any one or more of the devisees to the property, and the approval of the testator's will is not intended to effect in any way the restrictions as provided in the patents to the lands involved.

EB Meritt
Assistant Commissioner

Department of The Interior
Office of The Secretary   JUN 30 1920

The within will of Harry Whitebird, deceased Quapaw allottee 22-25 dated December 5, 1919, is hereby approved in accordance with the Act of June 25, 1910 (36 Stats. L., 855-6) as amended by Act of February 14, 1913 (37 Stats. L., 678) excepting as to the executor indicated therein and no rights of an executor are recognized. The approval of this will shall not be construed as a relinquishment of, or militate against the supervision of the United States Government over unpartitioned[sic] inherited lands, or those held under restricted fee, devised therein, and the rents, royalties and revenues derived therefrom, if such supervision is required by the status of any one or more of the devisees to the property, and the approval of the testator's will is not intended to effect in any way the restrictions as provided in the patents to the lands involved.

SG Hopkins
Assistant Secretary

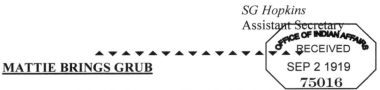

MATTIE BRINGS GRUB

OFFICE OF INDIAN AFFAIRS
RECEIVED
SEP 2 1919
75016

BE IT REMEMBERED THAT I, Mattie Brings Grub, Cheyenne River Sioux Allottee No. 1771, aged forty-eight years, being of sound and disposing mind and memory, do hereby publish, make and declare this as and for my last Will and Testament, hereby revoking all other Wills or Codicils heretofore made by me.

FIRST, to my husband, Paul Brings Grub, I hereby give, devise and bequeath, out of any moneys accruing to my estate, the sum of One Dollar.

SECOND, to my three children, Gideon Brings Grub, Lucy Brings Grub, and Paul Brings Grub, Jr., I give devise and bequeath all of my personal property, including one wagon, one harness, and two horses, in equal shares.

THIRD, To my three children, Gideon Brings Grub, Lucy Brings Grub, and Paul Brings Grub, Jr., I give devise and bequeath the following real estate; to be divided among them in equal shares:
My own allotment, described as the South Half (S1/2) of Section Sixteen (16), Township Thirteen (13) North, of Range Twenty-eight (28) East of the Black Hills Meridian.

My four ninths (4/9) inherited interest in the estate of my Father, Thomas Head, Cheyenne River Sioux allottee No. P.13-33; said allotment being described as West Half (W1/2) Section Eight (8) Township Four (4) North of Range Thirty-one (31) East B.H.M. and South Half (S1/2) Section Five (5), Township Four (4) North of Range Thirty-one (31) Eat B.H.M.

My One third (1/3) inherited interest in the estate of my other Lizzie Head, Cheyenne River Sioux allottee No. 2740, said estate consisting of allotment described as South Half (S1/2) Section Fifteen (15), Township Thirteen (13) North of Range Twenty-eight (28) East B.H.M.

IN WITNESS WHEREOF I have hereunto set my hand and seal this Nineteenth day of June 1919, at Cheyenne Agency, S.D. in the presence of two attesting witnesses.

(SEAL)   *Mattie Brings Grub*

THE FOREGOING WILL WAS SIGNED, SEALED, PUBLISHED AND DECLARED AS AND for her last Will and Testament by the said Mattie Brings Grub, and at her request and in her presence, and in the presence of each other we have hereunto subscribed our names as attesting witnesses this day and year first above mentioned.

Mrs. Fred La Plant   *Lizzie Tin Cup*
Cheyenne Agency, S.D.   Cheyenne Agency, S.D.

Department of the Interior,
Office of Indian Affairs, Washington,

JUN -2 1920

It is recommended that the within will be approved pursuant to the provisions of the Act of June 25, 1910 (36 Stats. L. 855-6) as amended by Act of February 14, 1913 (37 Stats. L. 678).

Respectfully,
EB Meritt
Assistant Commissioner

Department of The Interior
Office of The Secretary, Washington

The within will is hereby approved pursuant to the provisions of the Act of June 25, 1910 (36 Stats. L. 855-6) as amended by Act of February 14, 1913 (37 Stats. L. 678).

SG Hopkins
Assistant Secretary

ROBERT GREGORY

RECEIVED
AUG 12 1918
67385 GREENVILLE INDIAN SCHOOL, CALIF

RECEIVED
AUG 6 1918

I, Robert Gregory, being of sound mind, and knowing the uncertainty of this present life, do hereby make this my last will and testament.

I give and bequeat[sic] all of my property, personal and real, of whatsoever nature, to my wife, Sadie Gregory, that I am possessed of at the time of my death, excepting that which is necessary to pay any and all just debts that I may at that time owe.

It is my desire that all just debts that I may owe at the time of my death, be paid out of any money that I may be possessed of at the time of my death.

Signed *Robert Gregory*

We certify that the above was signed and sealed by the testator in our presence, and that we hereby witness his signature at his request.

Name   *D. H. Biggs*
Address *Baird, Cal*

Witnesses, -

Name   *H. F. Roller*
Address *Redding, Cal.*

Department of The Interior,
Office of Indian Affairs, Washington,

The within will of Robert Gregory is hereby recommended for approval in accordance with the Act of June 25, 1910 (36 Stats. L., 855-6) as amended by Act of February 14, 1913 (37 Stats. L., 678).

Respectfully,
CF Hawke
Acting Assistant Commissioner

Department of The Interior
Office of The Secretary   JUN 15 1920

The within will is hereby approved according to the provisions of the Act of June 25, 1910 (36 Stats. L., 855-6) as amended by Act of February 14, 1913 (37 Stats. L., 678).

SG Hopkins
Assistant Secretary

▲▼▲▼▲▼▲▼▲▼▲▼▲▼▲▼

RISING HAIL or WASUINAPE

LAST WILL AND TESTAMENT
of
RISING HAIL or WASUINAPE,
Yankton Sioux Allottee No. 678.

OFFICE OF INDIAN AFFAIRS
RECEIVED
APR 19 1920
33436

I, Rising Hail or Wasuinape, Yankton Sioux Allottee No. 678, of Greenwood, South Dakota, a ward of the United States Government, being of sound and disposing mind and memory, do make publish and declare this to be my last will and testament, hereby revoking all former will[sic] by me made:

First,   I give and devise to my only daughter and apparent heir, Rachel Patterson, that portion of my original allotment No. 678, described as follows: SW/4 of NW/4 and W/2 of SW/4 of Sec. 25, T 95 N, R 65 W., 5th P.M., in South Dakota, containing 120 acres.

Second,   I give and devise to my grandson, John Patterson, that portion of my original allotment No. 678, described as follows: SE/4 of NE/4 of Sec. 26, T. 95 N. R 65 W., 5th P.M., in South Dakota, containing 40 acres.

Third,   I give and devise to my grandson, Joseph Patterson, that portion of my original allotment No. 678, described as follows: NE/4 of SE/4 of Sec. 26, T 95 N. R. 65 W., 5th P.M., in South Dakota, containing 40 acres.

Fourth,   I give and devise to my grandson, Pinkpaduta, who is the oldest child of my daughter, Rachel Patterson and Understanding

Crow, being about 5 years of age at this time, that portion of my original allotment No. 678, described as follows: SE/4 of SE/4 of Sec. 26, T. 95 N. R. 65 W., 5th P.M., in South Dakota, containing 40 acres.

Fifth,   It is my desire that the rest and residue of my trust property remaining at the time of my decease shall descend to my heirs at law as may be determined by the Secretary of the Interior, and that there shall be no appeal from his findings as I do not want my relatives on the Rosebud Reservation to have any of my property.

IN TESTIMONY WHEREOF, I have hereunto subscribed my name and affixed my seal this 28th day of August, 1917.

WITNESSES TO MARK: His
Moses Archambeau   RISING HAIL or WASUINAPE [thumb print]
AJ Cassidy   mark

THE FOREGOING INSTRUMENT, Signed, Sealed, and Acknowledged by said testator, Rising Hail or Wasuinape, and by him published and declared to be his last will and testament in our presence, who, at his request, and in his presence, and in the presence of each other, have subscribed our names as witnesses hereto, this 28th day of August, 1917.

Witnesses to Will: Post Office Address:

Moses Archambeau   *Greenwood, S. Dak.*
A J Cassidy   *Wagner, S.D.*

Department of The Interior,
Office of Indian Affairs, Washington,
                        JUN -4 1920
It is hereby recommended that the within will be approved pursuant to the provisions of the Act of June 25, 1910 (36 Stats. L., 855-6) as amended by Act of February 14, 1913 (37 Stats. L., 678).

                              Respectfully,
                              EB Meritt
                              Assistant Commissioner

Department of The Interior
Office of The Secretary   JUN -9 1920

The within will is hereby approved pursuant to the provisions of the Act of June 25, 1910 (36 Stats. L., 855-6) as amended by Act of February 14, 1913 (37 Stats. L., 678).

SG Hopkins
Assistant Secretary

▲▼▲▼▲▼▲▼▲▼▲▼▲▼▲▼

MARY AM-YOW-ET

WILL

IN THE NAME OF GOD, AMEN. I, MARY Am-Yow-et, an American Indian residing on the Yakima Indian Reservation of about eighty (80) years of age, the person referred to in that Patent or allotment certificate bearing date July 10, 1897, executed by Wm McKinley, president of the United States, recorded in Volume 53 at page 446 of the records of the Department of the Interior, in which she was allotted, the

North East quarter of the North East quarter of Section 18,
and the Northwest quarter of the Northwest quarter of Section
17, in Township 12 North of Range eighteen (18) East
of the Willamette Meridian in Washington, County of Yakima,
and containing 80 acres,

and being of sound and disposing mind and memory and not acting under duress, menace, fraud or undo[sic] influence of any person whatsoever to make publish and declare this my last Will and Testament in manner following, that is to say:

1.

I direct that my body be decently buried.

2.

I direct that my executor or executors pay my funeral expenses and my last expenses of sickness.

3.

I give, devise and bequeath to my beloved friend and husband, Captain Joe, an American Indian now living with me, the East half of the Northeast quarter of the Northeast quarter of Section 18, Township 12, north of Range 18, East of Willamette Meridian in Yakima County, Washington, together with all heriditaments[sic] and appurtenances thereunto belonging or in any wise appurtaining[sic]: To have and to hold the same to the said Captain Joe, his heirs and assigns, forever.

4.

I give devise and bequeath to my beloved daughter Catherine Smartlowat an American Indian, now residing with me:

The West half of the Northeast quarter of the Northeast quarter of Section 18, and all of the Northwest quarter of the Northwest quarter of Section 17, all in Township 12, north of Range 18 East of Willamette Meridian, in Yakima County, Washington, containing 60 acres more or less,

together with all the heriditaments[sic] and appurtenances thereunto belonging or in any wise appurtaining[sic]: To have and to hold the same to the said Catherine Smartlowat, her heirs and assigns forever.

Also the Southwest quarter of the Northeast quarter and southeast quarter of the Northwest quarter of Section 18, township 12, north of Range 18, E.W.M. of Yakima County, Washington, containing eighty (80) acres more or less.

5.

I hereby declare and state that I have no other children living.

6.

I give, devise and bequeath all the rest of the residue and the remainder of my real, personal or mixed estate, goods and chattels of whatsoever kind or nature, owned by me at the time of my death, or in which I may have any interest, to my said beloved daughter Catherine Smartlowat.

I hereby lastly nominate and appoint, .*(Blank)* of ...*(Blank)*..... the executor of this my last Will and Testament, and I hereby revoke all former Wills by me made.

IN WITNESS WHEREOF I have hereunto set my hand and seal this *29th* day of October, A.D. 1918.

her

Mary [thumb print] Am-Yow-et

mark

Witness to her mark.

    Joseph Smartlowat

    Cecelia Andy

The foregoing instrument was at the date thereof, by the said Mary Am-Yow-et, signed and sealed and published and declared to be her Last Will and Testament in the presence of us at her request, and in her presence and in the presence of each other, we saw her execute the same by making her mark as thereon indicated and have subscribed our names as witnesses thereto.

(No Signature Given)

(No Signature Given)

Department of The Interior,
Office of Indian Affairs, Washington,

June 16, 1920

It is hereby recommended that the within will of Mary Amyowet, deceased Yakima allottee No. 925, be approved under the provisions of the Act of June 25, 1910 (36 Stats. L., 855-6) as amended by Act of February 14, 1913 (37 Stats. L., 678), and the Regulations of the Department.

Respectfully,

EB Meritt

Assistant Commissioner

Department of The Interior
Office of The Secretary   JUN 24 1920

The within will of Mary Amyowet, deceased Yakima allottee No. 925, is hereby approved under the provisions of the Act of June 25, 1910 (36 Stats. L., 855-6) as amended by Act of February 14, 1913 (37 Stats. L., 678), and the Regulations of the Department.

SG Hopkins

Assistant Secretary

▲▼▲▼▲▼▲▼▲▼▲▼▲▼▲

<u>NANCY GANGRO</u>

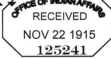

OFFICE OF INDIAN AFFAIRS
RECEIVED
NOV 22 1915
125241

W I L L

Spokane Indian Agency,
Lincoln, Wash. Oct. 16, 1914.

I, the undersigned, Nancy Gangro, being of sound mind and infirm body, realizing the uncertainty of human life, and desiring to despose[sic] of my possessions according to desert, do hereby will and bequeath, all my real property consisting of the West Half of the South West Quarter of Section Twenty Four (24) Township Twenty Nine (29) Range Thirty Six (36) E.W.M. and the Eat Half of the East Half of the East Half of the South East Quarter of Section twenty three (23) Township Twenty Nine (29) Range thirty six (36) E.W.M. in the State of Washington, in all One Hundred (100) acres, to Mrs. and Mrs. Tom Stengar of Tekoa, Washington, my niece and her husband, to have and to hold in perfect title, subject to the trust of the United States, after my decease.

My reason for this bequest is due to my gratitude to these persons for their kindness to me and the fact that they now propose to care for me in my helpless condition for the remainder of my natural life.

IN WITNESS WHEREOF, I have this day set my hand and seal.

her

Witnesses.   _Nancy Gangro_ [thumb print] _left_
  GM Peavy Tehra Washington   _thumb mark_
  Julia Brown Milo, Wash.

Department of The Interior,
Office of Indian Affairs, Washington,
JUN 29 1920

The within will of Nancy Gangro, deceased allottee No. 160 of the Shoshone Tribe, is respectfully recommended for approval pursuant to the provisions of the Act of June 25, 1910 (36 Stats. L., 855-6) as amended by Act of February 14, 1913 (37 Stats. L., 678).

EB Meritt
Assistant Commissioner

178

Department of The Interior
Office of The Secretary JUN 30 1920

The within will of Nancy Gangro is hereby approved in accordance with the Act of June 25, 1910 (36 Stats. L., 855-6) as amended by Act of February 14, 1913 (37 Stats. L., 678).

SG Hopkins
Assistant Secretary

▲▼▲▼▲▼▲▼▲▼▲▼▲▼▲▼